**MatarProductions:**
**MatarTV**
**MatarEducation**
**MatarPodcast**
*Stand August 2019*

Ali Matar

Lebanese 101:
The Easy Way to Learn Lebanese Arabic

The Ultimate Guide to Become a Lebanese

Map from *Nations Online Project.*

The Ultimate Guide to Become a Lebanese

## Table of Contents

**Introduction** .......................................................................... 3

**Chapter I Basics before Learning Lebanese Arabic 101** .............. 7

   Mistakes to Avoid while Learning Lebanese Arabic ................. 7

   Tips on Learning Lebanese Arabic Fast ................................. 10

   Get to know Lebanon ............................................................ 14

**Chapter II Learning Lebanese Arabic 101** ................................ 26

   Pronunciation guide and Arabic letters in Internet Language 26

   Subject Pronouns .................................................................. 29

   Definite Article ..................................................................... 35

   Demonstrative pronouns ...................................................... 37

   Yes & No ............................................................................... 41

   And ....................................................................................... 46

   Arabic numerals ................................................................... 47

   Possessive Pronouns ............................................................ 53

   Time-Telling .......................................................................... 61

   Colors ................................................................................... 69

   Days and Months ................................................................. 74

   Verb Conjugations ................................................................ 80

   Past Tense ............................................................................ 86

   The Imperfect Tense ............................................................ 89

   The Bi-Imperfect .................................................................. 91

   Future Tense ........................................................................ 93

Comparative/Superlative ........................................................ 95
Compound Tenses .................................................................. 98
Clothing ................................................................................... 99
Professions ........................................................................... 103
The Human Body .................................................................. 108
Relatives ............................................................................... 112
Verb Conjugations Examples ............................................... 117
**Chapter III Vocabulary: Lebanon Survival Pack ..................... 121**
Outro ..................................................................................... 134

# Introduction

## What is this book about?

**Let's start with the Fusha and the dialects, shall we?**

The Spoken Arabic is divided into formal and informal. The formal uses standard Arabic "Fusha" and the informal is a dialect that changes depending on the country. The dialects spoken are not written. The closer the dialect to standard Arabic, the easier for other people to understand it. That's why a Moroccan can understand an Iraqi, but the Iraqi can't understand a Moroccan (except for the few words here and there).

The reason however, as to why dialects differ from standard Arabic is due to the vowel system Arabic has. Vowels are not written. You have to instinctively guess what vowels there are (that comes with practise and knowing the context). So, changing one vowel can alter the meaning considerably, thus dialects were created. We also can define dialects as alteration of original vowel assigned to words, adding new words that is arabized during the period of colonization.

This book deals with the Lebanese Arabic. Lebanese Arabic or simply Lebanese is a variety of North Levantine Arabic, indigenous to and spoken primarily in Lebanon, with significant linguistic influences borrowed from other Middle Eastern and European languages and is in some ways unique from other varieties of Arabic. Due to multilingualism among Lebanese people (a majority of the Lebanese people are bilingual or trilingual), it is not uncommon for Lebanese people to mix Lebanese Arabic, English and French into their daily speech.

Lebanese Arabic shares many features with other modern varieties of Arabic. Lebanese Arabic, like many other spoken Levantine Arabic varieties, has a syllable structure very different from that of Modern Standard Arabic. While Standard Arabic can have only one consonant at the beginning of a syllable, after which a vowel must follow, Lebanese Arabic commonly has two consonants in the onset.

The idea of the book was born, when I started getting Emails and DMs on Instagram about my audience wanting me to translate my videos on YouTube to English. It turned out that although they are Lebanese, their parents have migrated a long time ago to either Europe, Australia or America and stayed there. Their parents could speak Lebanese, however, them not so much.

They tried learning Arabic, but all they could find was the traditional standard Arabic courses, which didn't help them at all.

As a Lebanese that learned the German language from zero, I knew exactly what my audience (now students) needed and wanted. It started with one Udemy course, then two, then three. A high demand is there as well for the fourth one, yet I decided to write this book instead and postpone the fourth course for later.

I hope this book will bring you the value to re-discover your Lebanese roots or to bring you closer to your Lebanese partner/family.

## What are the differences between the Standard Arabic and Lebanese Arabic?

Lebanese is a language that is primarily influenced by Phoenician Canaanite, Aramaic, Punic and Arabic. Those, along with other languages like Turkish, French, English, etc, make up what is today Lebanese.

That is other than the phonetic, phonological, semantic, syntactical and even morphological aspects that are either innovations or due to influences from different languages other than Arabic.

Other than that, more than half of the words we speak are not present in Arabic.

Arabic is learned at school and it is not even the primary language. French and English are much more important. Even in Arabic class, you're not expected to speak MSA, whereas in science classes you're not expected to speak other than French or English.

Interestingly, nobody speaks Arabic. Arabic is a written language and not a spoken one.

Example:

Get a rural Iraqi, a rural Yemeni, a rural Somali, a rural Lebanese, a rural Egyptian, a rural Algerian, and a rural Mauritanian, none of whom had the privilege to learn MSA. Yes, these are from every single region of the 'Arabic' world.

Put them in the same room and ask them to communicate.

It will be like putting a Portuguese and an Englishman together. Will they understand a few things? You bet they will. Will it be productive and will they save each other's lives? No, they will die in the room because they don't know how to communicate past a few words.

You could still tell yourself that it's the same language, however, according to the dictionary, a language is: "the method of human communication, either spoken or written, consisting of the use of words in a structured and conventional way." and/or "The system of communication used by a particular community or country."

If you cannot communicate, you do not speak the same language.

Period.

So, let's start learning.

*Adapted from: https://www.quora.com/What-are-the-differences-between-the-Arabic-and-Lebanese-languages*

# Chapter I
# Basics before Learning Lebanese Arabic 101

### Mistakes to Avoid while Learning Lebanese Arabic

Arabic is considered to be one of the most difficult languages in the world to learn. In fact, it is one of the 'big three' languages which require the most time and commitment from students if they want to truly master it. If you're ready to put in the hard work it takes to learn Arabic, then you definitely don't want to waste time trying to correct common mistakes. Learning what these mistakes are, can help you avoid them and give you an advantage, many other students may not have. So, read on to discover 6 common mistakes learners of Arabic tend to make.

**1. Not knowing the difference between Classical Arabic and Spoken Arabic:**

Unlike languages such as French or German, when you learn Arabic you are typically learning more than one language. Classical Arabic is the written form of the language and this style is rarely used in day-to-day speech. Spoken Arabic, on the other hand, should be used in regular verbal interactions. Knowing which is which is a key step in being able to successfully learn Arabic!

**2. Not knowing your end goal:**

Not setting an end goal when you start learning Arabic can be detrimental to the learning process because you'll end up jumping all over the place as opposed to focusing on a single language path. If complete fluency is your goal, then you should focus on Spoken Arabic. However, if you plan on using Arabic purely for academic or religious purposes, you can hone your focus in on Classical Arabic. Likewise, if you will use it mainly for business, travel, and living abroad, then Spoken Arabic should be your aim.

### 3. Not finding a language tutor:

While it is possible to learn some languages purely through self-study, Arabic is not one of those. A big mistake many Arabic learners make is that they believe they can first learn Arabic alone and then put it to use later. Unfortunately, Arabic's tricky pronunciation makes this learning method completely useless. You'll need to find a qualified instructor who can guide you in the right direction and help you develop those speaking skills.

### 4. Not practicing speaking every day:

Pronunciation is one of the key things which can make Arabic so challenging to learn. Many Arabic words have a back-of-the-throat (or guttural) way that they are pronounced. This is very challenging to many learners as Latin-based languages rarely put the throat to use in such a way. Spend at least 15 minutes a day talking aloud to yourself in Arabic. This will help your tongue and throat to become accustomed to the pronunciation. And, of course, find someone (preferably a native speaker) who can correct your speech and help you to improve it.

### 5. Not having realistic goals:

It is important to be realistic when you're setting goals in your Arabic language learning journey. This is, after all, a language which will take you at least 2200 hours (88 weeks) or more to master, and this isn't even taking into account the different dialects you'll have to learn in order to communicate in Egypt,

Saudi Arabia, or Syria! Your language tutor can also help you set realistic goals, whether it is talking to yourself for 15 minutes a day, or learning 10 new vocabulary words a week. Setting realistic aims will make you feel like you really are accomplishing something as opposed stuck in a stalemate with your language learning.

**6. Not approaching Arabic differently:**

Many students make the mistake of approaching Arabic the way they would other 'easier' languages such as French or Spanish. They expect to progress at the same rate as they would with these other tongues and end up falling short, feeling disappointed with themselves or even worse, giving up on learning Arabic altogether. Approach Arabic with care, realize that it may take you longer to achieve things with this language than with others and above all, be patient and kind to yourself. Committing to learning a new language already makes you a winner!

## Tips on Learning Lebanese Arabic Fast

**1. You don't need to attempt to learn Modern Standard Arabic:**

As mentioned before in this book. Modern Standard Arabic is not spoken by anyone on earth as a native language. If you want to learn MSA then go for it, however, if you want to learn to speak Arabic, then learning a dialect is the way for you to go.

MSA might and will in some cases contradict what you want to learn in the spoken Arabic. Arabic is confusing enough. So, keep it simple and choose a dialect (like Lebanese) to learn.

**2. Practice the importance of Acculturation and Assimilation from the beginning:**

The one thing that a lot of people forget to recognize is that when you're learning a language, you're not only learning this language alone, you're getting to know the culture as well.

Fluency only comes about when you're fluent in the culture as well (not literally).

If you don't respect and appreciate the culture and its people, then don't waste your time.

And if you want to truly excel in any language, *strive to assimilate*.

**3. Surround yourself with people speaking the dialect:**

Be more active in finding every single opportunity to be around Lebanese people. Try to attend every event there is. You have no idea how many people you might get to know and even become close friends with!

Find teachers that teach with a communicative style:

Traditional learning methods do not work anymore. Sadly, a lot of Arabic teachers still stick to those old methods and teach you MSA as if it still matters. Find teacher that focus on teaching the dialect.

You might come across teachers that are boring and are in it only for the money. Don't mind them. Try to find another new fun teacher!

**4. Start speaking Arabic as soon as possible, even better when you make mistakes:**

I know what you feel. I speak 3 languages, Arabic (duh), English and German. Was I born fluent in all 3? No sir. It took practice and perseverance. Did I make mistakes? Hell yea! I made so many mistakes you can't even imagine. Heck, even in this book there are some grammatical mistakes I am sure of that. Did that affect anything? Well, I hope not. However, I still try and will keep on trying to bring you value. So, don't be shy doing mistakes. You should make mistakes in order to improve. Don't be shy to even ask your friends to correct you! I am sure they will be glad to do that for you.

**5. Spend time using quality books and resources:**

Time for self-promotion. Hehe.

Everything started when I first began my YouTube career. My niche became Lebanese people from Lebanon and also worldwide. I kept being asked where they can learn Lebanese Arabic. Sadly, there was no good platform for this. So, I decided I want to bring value to my fans and audience.

I first made a beginner course for teaching the Lebanese dialect on Udemy and launched it. It exploded.

Now, I have three Udemy courses with over 750 Students and they are loving it.

You can check here for yourselves:

 Terry Zhou 2 weeks ago

I loved this beginner's course with Ali! He's an amazing teacher and he really makes his videos fun and entertaining to watch. He also adds extra homework for each lesson to help you practice on the material he just teaches. As a non arabic speaker, I learned a lot from him and I'm really satisfied with my purchase.

Learn The Spoken Arabic Language (Lebanese Ar...

 Anastasiia Cherkasova 11 hours ago

It is once of the best and most effective courses in Lebanese Arabic I managed to find after trying hundreds of sources! Mumtaaz!

Learn The Spoken Arabic Language (Lebanese Ar...

And also, these recent feedbacks from my students:

⭐⭐⭐⭐⭐
Kindal Al Arnaout  1 day ago
Learn The Spoken Arabic Language (Lebanese Arabic)

⭐⭐⭐⭐⭐
Jarrod Young  4 days ago
Learn The Spoken Arabic Language (Lebanese Arabic)

⭐⭐⭐⭐⭐
Richard Caldwell  4 days ago
Learn The Spoken Arabic Language (Lebanese Arabic)

⭐⭐⭐⭐⭐
Maya Bou Khalil  4 days ago
Learn The Spoken Arabic Language (Lebanese Arabic)

⭐⭐⭐⭐⭐
Sanaa Elhosni  5 days ago
Learn The Spoken Arabic Language (Lebanese Arabic)

All of my courses could be found underneath every description of every video I have on YouTube: MatarTV, MatarEducation and MatarPodcast.

You can also send me an Email or just DM me on Instagram under the name: MatarTV

I also offer 24/7 WhatsApp customer service, in case you have any questions regarding the book or even a question about the Lebanese dialect!

Use this link over here: https://wa.me/4915201448711

Or try adding this number: +4915201448711

I hope you will enjoy this book and I will be looking forward for us to meet in Beirut someday and speak ONLY in Lebanese!

Stay well Habibis and have fun!

# Get to know Lebanon

As I mentioned before, getting to know the culture will help your language learning process. However, if you feel you know everything about Lebanon, then feel free to skip the culture chapter. I just don't carry the responsibility on what you might miss on!

## Orientation

**Identification:** *Libnen* derives from the Phoenician for "white mountain" and denotes Lebanon's mountains, some parts of which remain snow-covered all year.
**Location and Geography:** Lebanon is bounded on the north and east by Syria, on the west by the Mediterranean and on the south by Palestine.

Lebanon consists of two mountain chains, the Lebanon and the ante-Lebanon; a narrow coastal strip, where all the major cities lie; and a fertile plain, the Bekaa valley, which lies between the two mountain chains and provides most of the local agricultural produce.

The capital, Beirut, was chosen for its ideal location on the Mediterranean and acts as the heart of Lebanon's banking industry, tourism and trade. The port of Beirut is the busiest and most important in the country.

**Demography:** The **population of Lebanon** is estimated at 6.86 million in **2019**, up from the 4.43 million estimated in 2013, which makes it the 108th most populated country in the world. The birth rate in Lebanon is 14.3 births/1,000 population and the death rate is 5 per thousand (2017 est.). The average life expectancy for those born at the end of the twentieth century was 69.35 years.

At independence, gained in 1943, the population was one-half Christian and one-half Muslim, a higher birth rate among Shiite Muslims upset this balance and was one of the causes of the civil war. Estimates in the 1990s (after the civil war) reveal a population composed of nearly 70 percent Muslims and 30 percent Christians. As of 2019, estimates of the population are as follows, Muslim 54% (27% Sunni, 27% Shia), Christian 40.5% (includes 21% Maronite Catholic, 8% Greek Orthodox, 5% Greek Catholic, 6.5% other Christian), Druze 5.6%, very small numbers of Jews, Baha'is, Buddhists, Hindus and Mormons.

**Linguistic Affiliation:** Languages spoken include Arabic, French, English, and Armenian. There are many accents in Lebanon. The Beirut accent is the mellowest and most highly regarded, while country accents are harsher. Accents are a much higher indicator of social status.

Lebanon has seen many invasions, which introduced new cultures and languages. The Canaanites, the first known settlers in the country, spoke a Semitic language. In the Hellenistic era Greek was introduced and spoken along with Aramaic. Latin later became common and finally the Arab invasion in the eighth century introduced and assured the hegemony of Arabic. Today, all Lebanese speak Arabic; most of them, especially the upper and middle classes, speak French. Nowadays, English has become as equally important as French.

The country's religious diversity has led to the transformation of many religious holidays into national ones. Additionally, the new government has placed much emphasis on secular holidays, particularly*Id Il-Jaysh*, which celebrates the accomplishments of the Lebanese Army.

**Symbolism:** The cedar in the center of the Lebanese flag is the symbol of six thousand years of history: the cedar was Lebanon's chief export in ancient times. The location of the cedar tree in the middle of the flag touching the upper and lower red stripes is also a reminder of Lebanon's constant troubles because the red stripes represent the blood spilt by the Lebanese throughout their history.

## Urbanism and Architecture

Most of Lebanon's population lives in the main cities of Beirut, Tripoli and Sidon which are densely populated.

Cities in Lebanon suffer from a lack of space. Most people live in apartments. Furniture is often a mixture of Arabic, Italian, European, and American styles. Apartments are usually decorated in western style: couches are placed against the walls and walls are often adorned with framed paintings and tapestries.

Lebanese people gather for sports, political events and concerts. The Lebanese prefer to hold public gatherings in open-air and historical locations.

Government buildings are generally simple and do not display reliefs, paintings, or slogans. Government buildings are often surrounded with small flowerbeds and/or trees.

## Food and Economy

**Food in Daily Life:** Lebanese cuisine is Mediterranean. Pita bread is a primary. The Lebanese enjoy *hummus* (a chickpea dip), *fool* (a fava bean dip) and other bean dishes. Rice is nearly a primary and pasta is very popular. Salted yogurt is common in many dishes. Red meat and chicken are common but are usually eaten as part of a dish. Pork is less popular, since it is forbidden under Islamic law.

Eating in Lebanon is tied to family: people almost never eat alone. The Lebanese consider eating out a social and almost aesthetic experience. Hence, restaurants usually have a pleasant view, of which Lebanon's geography affords many.

**Food Customs at Ceremonial Occasions:** *Ramadan*, the Muslim month of fasting, is the occasion for large meals at sundown. Soup, *fatteh* (a chick pea and yogurt dish) and *karbooj* (a nut-rich pastry) are especially eaten during Ramadan.

During Lent, Christians eat meatless dishes and at Barbara (Halloween) they eat a variety of wheat-based dishes.

**Basic Economy:** Although Lebanon produces and exports much of its agricultural produce, it still imports much of what its inhabitants consume, such as rice and some vegetables. Since most people live in city apartments, the only Lebanese who grow their own food live in mountain villages and some coastal towns.

**Land Tenure and Property:** Private property is very common and encouraged in Lebanon, although the government still owns most public services. Land laws are similar to those in France and the United States, but both religious and secular courts govern land inheritance.

**Commercial Activities:** Lebanon produces and sells oranges, apples and other fruits, as well as a variety of beans and vegetables. It is also becoming a Middle East hub for a number of computer software and hardware manufacturers. The banking industry, which was very prominent before the war, is once again rising to occupy a privileged place in the region.

**Major Industries:** The major industry is the manufacture of concrete and building material, to serve local needs. There are also some small factories that produce clothing and fabrics.

**Trade:** Lebanon sells fruits and vegetables to neighbouring Arab countries as well as to Italy, France and the United States. Wine is produced in the Bekaa and exported to France. Lebanon imports fruits and vegetables from Europe, North Africa and the Middle East; crude oil from Saudi Arabia and Kuwait; electric and electronic gadgets and cars from Europe, Japan, and North America.

**Division of Labor:** Adolescents in Lebanon rarely work. The working population is usually 18 years and older. Lebanon is mainly a capitalist country and the price of living is quite high.

Construction companies prefer to hire workers from Syria or Egypt, who will accept a wage of about $100 (U.S.) a month, an insufficient wage for a Lebanese.

## Social Stratification

**Classes and Castes:** Money is now the most important factor in determining class lines. The middle class suffered a great loss of wealth during the war and the gap between the very rich upper class and the lower class has widened. As a result, there have been numerous strikes and demonstrations. Differences in wealth and status often occur along religious and family lines.

**Symbols of Social Stratification:** All Christians and most Muslims who live in the cities wear European style clothes. In poorer Muslim towns and in some Muslim areas in the main cities, one may still find the Muslim *chador* (the veil traditional Muslim women wear). In the countryside, women sometimes wear traditional colourful skirts and men wear a traditional *sherwal* (baggy trousers).

## Political Life

**Government:** Lebanon is a democratic republic with a parliament, a cabinet and a president, although power is divided along religious lines. The President (a Maronite Catholic), who lost part of his executive power after the war, is the head of state; the Prime Minister (a Sunni Muslim) is the head of government and chairs the Cabinet; the Speaker of the House (a Shiite Muslim) presides over Parliament, which passes the Cabinet's bills and elects the President.

**Social Problems and Control:** Lebanese civil law is based on the French Napoleonic law. Police as well as the Forces of General Security uphold the law on the streets. People rarely take the law into their own hands, except when it came to opposing ideologies during the civil war.

**Military Activity:** The Lebanese Army was highly divided along religious lines during the civil war. Today, the government has rebuilt the army and modernized it.

## Social Welfare

Unemployment is high in Lebanon and at least according to the IMF and other international organizations, the government, which is struggling to rebuild the country's infrastructure, does not offer sufficient help for the unemployed.

## Gender Roles and Statuses

**Division of Labor by Gender:** The marketplace traditionally has favored men and more women stay at home than men. Women are allowed to vote, work, attend school and participate in all forms of public life, but they tend to occupy traditionally female jobs such as secretaries and school teachers.

**The Relative Status of Women and Men:** Men hold higher social status than women because of the omnipresence of patriarchal religions in Lebanese life. Family is still stressed, as is the woman's role as a nurturing mother. However, many women have broken traditional boundaries and entered the political, artistic, and literary environment, especially in Beirut and other major cities.

## Marriage, Family and Kinship

**Marriage:** Arranged marriages are rare, although they still exist. The country's present economic crisis has rendered money, a secure job and a home big factors in contracting marriages.

Polygamy is legal among Muslims; however, it holds a social stigma and very few people choose this lifestyle.

Religious courts decide on issues of marriage and divorce. Divorce is easy among Muslims, harder for Orthodox Christians and most difficult in Maronite communities. The divorce rate remains very low.

**Domestic Unit:** In the household, the husband and wife share authority, although wives usually wield more influence over children and in various household matters.

**Inheritance:** Inheritance laws are the affair of the various religious courts, which usually favours male heirs. In villages, land is the most important inheritance, whereas apartments, money, and privately-owned shops constitute the bulk of inheritance in the cities.

**Kin Groups:** After the family, a person's loyalty is usually with members of his/her own religion who inhabit the same town. However, marriage between different religious groups has become frequent and at the end of the twentieth century there was an effort to pass a law legalizing civil marriages which may undermine the traditional religious.

## Socialization

**Infant Care:** Kindergartens and babysitters are becoming more common as many women today work outside the house. Quite often grandparents or members of the extended family will help to care for a baby.

**Child Rearing and Education:** Education is very important in Lebanon. Many parents prefer to place their children in the more expensive religious private schools, where they may receive moral guidance.

Parents are usually strict and demand great devotion. Lebanese children grow up with deep respect for their parents.

**Higher Education:** Higher education is highly encouraged in Lebanon, which still has some of the best universities in the region. However, there are very few jobs awaiting young graduates.

## Etiquette

The Lebanese are very outgoing. The *souks* (markets) are always crowded; shopping downtown is very popular, as is strolling with friends along the busy streets. Lebanese people usually sit close together and interact vivaciously.

Manners are important and are highly influenced by French etiquette, especially in matters of dress, address, and eating. Strangers as well as acquaintances greet each other respectfully, usually using French terms, such as *bonjour, bonsoir,* and *pardon*.

Hospitality is very important. Travelers to Lebanon are received genially.

## Religion

**Religious Beliefs:** Most people in Lebanon are religious and monotheistic. Lebanon is made up of Muslim and Christian sects which escaped persecution throughout history by seeking shelter in its mountains. No one religion is dominant. The country has Muslim Shiites, Sunnis, Druzes, Christian Maronites, Greek Orthodox and Armenian Orthodox.

**Religious Practitioners:** Religious figures have a lot of authority in Lebanon since religious courts decide on many issues concerning individuals' rights and privileges. This authority has been slightly undermined by the civil war.

**Death and the Afterlife:** Funerals are usually very elaborate; people are encouraged to express their feelings of loss openly and to follow funeral processions.

All the religions in Lebanon place much emphasis on the afterlife. Individuals are constantly exhorted to live righteous lives in the present, which will allow them to enter a beauteous paradise.

## The Arts and Humanities

**Support for the Arts:** Artists are usually self-supporting, although some do receive contributions from patrons of the arts. There is no official government allocation of monies for the arts, although art schools sometimes receive government aid.

**Literature:** Lebanon has a long history of excellent poets and novelists. In the early years of the twentieth century, Lebanese authors took the lead in defending Arabic and its use in literary creation. Today, Lebanon still has many authors who write in Arabic as well as French and sometimes English.

Oral literature is preserved in villages, where the *zajal*, a form of poetic contest in the Lebanese dialect is alive and enjoyed by everyone.

**Graphic Arts:** Painting is very varied and encouraged in Lebanon. French surrealists, cubists, and impressionists mostly influence Lebanese artists, who add an oriental touch to the French technique and subject matter. Many exhibits are held throughout the country, including the recently reopened Lebanese Museum in Beirut.

Traditional pottery-making is still popular in the coastal towns, such as Al-Minaa in the north and Sidon in the south.

Local crafts are encouraged and many souks specialize in selling traditional objets d'art to tourists.

**Performance Arts:** Oriental and Western music are both popular. International festivals are once again very popular and offer an array of symphonies, classical and modern ballets, foreign and local dance troupes, opera and pop singers. These festivals are usually held in open air on historic sites, such as the Roman temples of Baalbek, Byblos' crusader ruins or Beirut's central district. Because of the diversity of the programs such festivals offer, people from all walks of life attend and interact.

## The State of the Physical and Social Sciences

Schools of engineering are highly developed in Lebanon. However, they produce more engineers than the country needs and many engineers find themselves unemployed or forced to accept menial jobs.

Social sciences are taught at the major universities; however, students are not encouraged to pursue them as they are less lucrative than other careers.

The Lebanese are encouraged to learn foreign languages and are usually bilingual.

*Adapted from: https://www.everyculture.com/Ja-Ma/Lebanon.html*

# Chapter II
# Learning Lebanese Arabic 101

## Pronunciation guide and Arabic letters in Internet Language

A new writing style spreads around the world, especially the Arab world; it's not Arabic or English. It's a mixture between both of them. It has its own name depending on the language by which person transliterate Arabic.

The broader phenomenon is known as **Franco Arab.**

The roots of this phenomenon go back to 1990 when the western text communication technologies became increasingly prevalent in the Arab world such as personal computers, cellular phones, emails and world wide webs. At that time, Arabic alphabet wasn't an optional feature and Latin alphabet was commonly used in all of these forms of communication. So, how could Arab users of this new western system communicate?

Written Arabic **has 28 letters**, some of them include sounds that are not used in English. Arabs had no choice but transliterating their Arabic into English using Latin letters. Not only letters were used in this process but also numbers because some Arabic letters don't have an approximate phonetic equivalent in Latin script. So, they used numerals and other characters to express their Arabic letters, e.g. number "3" is used to stand for the Arabic letter "ع" (Ayn) as they look alike.

**Franco Arabic** writing features:
*For pronunciation purposes, please check my YouTube channel:*
*MatarEducation*

| Letter | Arabic | Pronunciation | Explanation |
|---|---|---|---|
| 2 | ء | Glottal Stop | Like you're about to vomit but nothing comes out |
| Th/s | ث | Thh | The sound effect of a human being impersonating a snake (Throw) |
| 3 | ع | Ayn | |
| 5 | خ | Hh | Like DJ Khaled, but more a vulgar pronunciation |
| 7 | ح | Hh | When you have a sore throat |
| 8/gh | غ | Ghein | |

This new writing style on the internet became so popular, it is now used to express everyday speech. Many abbreviations for this speech are invented by the users.

**Note: It is really important that you take your time to learn and practice the pronunciations.**

Other abbreviations are made up for the most commonly used English expressions in Arab world:

| Full | Abbreviation |
| --- | --- |
| Laugh out loud | Lol |
| Welcome back | WB |
| Tomorrow | Tom |
| Today | 2day |
| Please | Plz |
| Before | B4 |
| Blackberry me | Bbm |
| Faecbook me | Fbm |
| How are you | Hru |
| How are things | Hrt |
| See you tomorrow | Cu tom |

**PS.** **This is a spoken language not a written one, so writings may differ if you check somewhere else or even later in this book.**

*Again, for pronunciation purposes, please check my YouTube channel: MatarEducation*

*Some info adapted from: https://arabeya.wordpress.com/2011/04/27/franco-3arabi/*

## Subject Pronouns

Also called **personal pronouns**. Arabic subject pronouns tell you who is doing the action of a sentence.

In English, subject pronouns are words such as "you", "we" and "it".

Arabic, is slightly more complicated, because it uses **gender** and **duality**. However, in Lebanese Arabic, duality is not commonly used, only the singularity and plurality are used. For example, "you" can be translated in different ways, depending on who you are talking to. In the case of talking to a singular male, it translates as "**2enta**", but for a singular female "**2ente**".

Normally, if you're talking to two males or two females, it becomes '2antoma'. However, this is not used in the Lebanese Arabic.

And finally, in the Arabic language, if you're talking to a group of three people or more with at least one male, "you" translates as (2antom) and for a group of three or more females (2anton). However, in the Lebanese Arabic, we use „**2ento**" for both males and females. (Life's easier when it's Lebanese Arabic right?)

PS. The subject pronoun "it" does not exist neither in official Arabic language nor the Lebanese Arabic.

| Subject Pronouns in English | Subject Pronouns in Lebanese Arabic |
| --- | --- |
| I | Ana |
| You (Male) | 2enta/Enta |
| You (Female) | 2ente/Ente |
| He | Howwe |
| She | Hiyye |
| We | Ne7na |
| You (Plural) | 2ento/Ento |
| They | Hinne |

Is and are, are auxiliary verbs that are mainly used in forming the tenses of other verbs.

In the Arabic language, there **are no auxiliary verbs.**

Example:

I am sick → Ana mareed. (I sick, which means I am sick)

*Ana: I*
*Mareed: sick*

The correct translation from English to Arabic would be: I ~~am~~ sick.

## How to figure out the gender of the noun:

As it has been mentioned before, in the Arabic language, there are feminine and masculine nouns. How do you differ between them? I will tell you a trick that works on almost all nouns.

I will make it as simple as possible:

**The nouns** ending with:

*-a/e are <u>feminine</u>*
*When the pronunciation (the sound)* **has a stop** *at the end, it's <u>masculine.</u>*

**Example:**

*Table: Tawle – feminine*
*Pen: 2alam – masculine*

*Paper: War2a – feminine*
*Door: Beb – masculine*

*Chapters specifically about nouns will be found later in the book. However, I would like to use some of the nouns already in some texts after some chapters to help you comprehend the idea faster.*

**Text:**

Mar7aba. Ana Jean. Howwe 5ayye w hiyye 2i5te. Ne7na 3anna bet. Fi 3anna jnayne kbire. Jiranna ktir mne7. Hinne 3andon Seyyara.

*Translation:*

*Hello. Ana jean. He is my brother and she is my sister. We have a house. We have a big garden. Our neighbors are really nice. They have a car.*

Nouns:

Bet: *House **(Masculine)***
Jnayne: *Garden **(Feminine)***
Seyyara: *Car **(Feminine)***


**Notes**

# Test

**Guess the gender of the following nouns:**

Ghinniyye *(Song):*
7a2i2a *(Truth):*
Marad *(Disease):*
Manta2a *(City or region):*
She22a *(Apartment):*
2a5bar *(News):*
7arara *(Temperature):*
3amar *(Construction):*
3asfoor *(Bird):*
2ossa *(Story):*
3a2ed *(Contract):*
Maktab *(Office):*
Sellom *(Ladder):*
Camera *(Camera):*
Jesh *(Army):*
Balad *(Country):*
Jareede *(Newspaper):*
Majalle *(Magazine):*
Mistashfa *(Hospital):*
Guitar *(Guitar):*
5otaab *(Speech):*

# Answers

Ghinniyye *(Song):* Feminine
7a2i2a *(Truth):* Feminine
Marad *(Disease):* Masculine
Manta2a *(City or region):* Feminine
She22a *(Apartment):* Feminine
2a5bar *(News):* Masculine
7arara *(Temperature):* Feminine
3amar *(Construction):* Masculine
3asfoor *(Bird):* Masculine
2ossa *(Story):* Feminine
3a2ed *(Contract):* Masculine
Maktab *(Office):* Masculine
Sellom *(Ladder):* Masculine
Camera *(Camera):* Feminine
Jesh *(Army):* Masculine
Balad *(Country):* Masculine
Jareede *(Newspaper):* Feminine
Majalle *(Magazine):* Feminine
Mistashfa *(Hospital):* Feminine
Guitar *(Guitar):* Masculine
5otaab *(Speech):* Masculine

## Definite Article

The Arabic definite article, corresponding to **"the"** in English, is composed of the letters *2alif + lām*. It is not an independent word, but is always prefixed to the noun or adjective it is defining. There is only this form of the definite article in Arabic, irrespective of the gender or number of the words being defined.

In Lebanese Arabic, **the letters 2alif + lām is pronounced *al* and written *L*.**

**Note** that there is **no indefinite article** in Arabic. Where English uses "**a**" or "**an**".

Arabic simply uses the singular form of the noun. Thus, *2istez* for example, can mean "teacher" or "a teacher".

Examples:

| Definite | |
|---|---|
| The teacher | L 2istez |
| The boy | L sabe |
| The tables | L tawlet |

| Indefinite | |
|---|---|
| (a) teacher | 2istez |
| (a) boy | Sabe |
| Tables | Tawlet |

All words with the definite article are definite; however, not all words **without it are indefinite**. Names of cities, countries, specific places or people – in short, anything that is a proper noun – are **definite** even if they do not have the definite article. Many proper nouns do, however, have the definite article, e.g. *Lba7ren* / Bahrain.

Example:

**L 2istez 7at l war2a 3ala l tawle.**
*The teacher put the paper on the table.*

*2istez: Masculine*
*War2a: Feminine*
*Tawle: Feminine*

**Notes**

_____
_____
_____
_____
_____
_____
_____
_____
_____
_____

## Demonstrative pronouns

As you know, in English there are two cases for demonstrative pronouns:

to point to a near object

- "**This**" is used to point to the near **singular** object.
- "**These**" is used to point towards the near **plural** objects.

to point to a distant object

- "**That**" is used for the distant (singular) object.
- "**Those**" is used for the distant (plural) objects.

And in Arabic, demonstrative pronouns are used in the same way as English demonstratives.

However, Arabic has many more demonstratives than English due to the masculine and feminine differentiation. In the standard Arabic also dual, but not in the Lebanese Arabic, as said before, the dual always becomes plural.

It is very important in Arabic to make sure that the demonstrative pronoun agrees with the noun it refers to in number, gender and case.

## Masculine Demonstrative Nouns:

The basic masculine singular demonstrative noun in Arabic is **Hayda**. **Hayda** is commonly used in spoken form of the Lebanese Arabic and is used to refer to a person, an animal, or an object that is **near** us, as in these examples:

This is an intelligent boy: *Hayda sabe zake*

This book is for Mohammad: *Hayda l kteb la Mohammad*

This pen is mine: *Hayda l 2alam la ele*

To refer to a person, an animal, or an object that is **fairly far** from us, we use **Haydak**. Here, **K** is added to the basic masculine singular demonstrative noun to indicate the distance (i.e. fairly far).

For example:

This is an intelligent boy and that is a good teacher: *Hayda sabe zake w haydak 2istez mnee7.*

This book is for Mohammad and that pen is for Elias: *Hayda l kteb la Mohammad w haydak l 2alam la Elias.*

This pen is mine and that pencil is yours: *Hayda l 2alam la ele w haydak l 2alam l rsas la elak.*

**Feminine Demonstrative Nouns:**

The basic feminine singular demonstrative noun in Arabic is **Hayde**. Unlike with the masculine, we replace the ‚a' with ‚e'. **Hayde** is commonly used in spoken form of Arabic. **Hayde** is used to refer to a person, an animal, or an object that is near us. The form of **Hayde** remains the same regardless of its position in the sentence, as in these examples:

This is a teacher (female): *Hayde m3alme*

This is a chicken: *Hayde djeje*

This is a school: *Hayde madrase*

To refer to a person, an animal, or an object that is fairly far from us, we use **Haydeek**.

For example:

That paper is for me: *Haydeek l war2a la ele*

That table is white: *Haydeek l tawle bayda*

**Notes**

_____
_____
_____
_____
_____
_____
_____
_____

## Plural Masculine and Feminine Demonstrative Nouns:

In the plural there are two forms: **Hole** and **Holeek**. The first is for people that are near us and the other is for people far from us. They have the same forms regardless of their position in the sentence, as in these examples:

These books: *Hole l kotob*
Those tables: *Holeek l tawlet*

I know these ladies: *Ba3rif hole l banet*
I know these guys: *Ba3rif hole l sobyen*

| - | Near | Far |
|---|---|---|
| Masculine | Hayda | Haydak |
| Feminine | Hayde | Haydeek |
| Plural | Hole | Holeek |

### Example:

**Hayde l kirse 3laya hayda l kteb**
*This chair has this book on it*

**Haydak l shab jeb haydeek l 2annine**
*That guy brought that bottle*

**Hole l kibbeyet byin7atto 7ad holeek l s7oon**
*These cups have to be placed next to those plates.*

## Yes & No

The words **'Yes'** and **'No'**, as little and as inconspicuous as they may be, are one of the most basic words anyone will ever learn to say whenever learning a new language. In Arabic it is no different. The word for **No** in Arabic is **'La2'** and the word for **Yes** in Arabic is **'2eh/eh'**, but just knowing these two isn't perfect right?

Whenever you're answering a question with a yes or no, you answer with either 'Please' or 'Thank you'.

We go back one more time to the gender. In Arabic, it depends if you're talking to a female or a male.

**Please** for a male: **3mol ma3roof.**
**Please** for a female: **3mele ma3roof.**

Thank you. Thank you doesn't necessarily refer to either a male or a female.

**Thank you: Shokran**

However, you can say:
Thank you to you (male): Shokran la elak
Thank you to you (female): Shokran le elik

## How to form "Yes/No" Questions

This is a pen         *Hayda 2alam*

Is this a pen?        *Hayda 2alam?*

This is a paper       *Hayde War2a*

Is this a paper?      *Hayde War2a?*

These are books       *Hole kotob*

Are these books?      *Hole kotob?*


**Remind**

**No = La2**

**Yes = 2eh/eh**

# Test

*Nouns to use for the exercise:*

*Pen: 2alam*
*Paper/Papers: War2a/wra2*
*Curtain: Birdeye*
*Chair/Chairs: Kirse/Karase*
*Table: Tawle*
*Door: Beb*
*Candle: Sham3a*

**Please answer the questions with yes or no using the right demonstrative nouns:**

| 1. Hayda 2alam? | 2. Hayde Tawle? |
|---|---|
| Eh, _____ . | La2, _____ . |

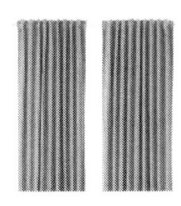

3. Hayde Sham3a?
_____.

4. Hole Karase?
_____

5. Sho hay?
_____.

6. Sho hayda?
_____.

## Answers

1. *Hayda 2alam*
2. *Hole wra2*
3. *La2, hayde birdeye*
4. *Eh, hole karase*
5. *Hayde tawle*
6. *Hayda beb*

**Notes**

## And

The letter **w** represents the article "**and**" in Lebanese.

1. It is normally pronounced as part of the second word.

Im **w** bay: *A mother and a father*

Kirse **w** ṫawle: *A chair and a table*

Bint **w** ṡabe: *A girl and a boy*

Jack **w** Sandra: *Jack and Sandra*

2. In case the word following "**w**" starts with a vowel, then "**w**" shall be pronounced as part of the previous word. A slight liaison might be felt between the end of the last word and the article "**w**".

Kteb **w** alam *(book and pen)*

Bay **w** imm *(dad and mom)*

Inta **w** ana *(you and me)*

3. Sometimes, a slight liaison is felt between the article **w** and the beginning of the second word. This normally occurs when the second word starts with two successive consonants, which means that the article w will make them three consonants in a row.

Alam **w** kteb is almost pronounced Alam **wi** kteb (pen and book)

kitob **w** zhur is almost pronounced kitob **wi** zhur (books and flowers)

# Arabic numerals

## Arabic numbering rules

**Digits from zero to nine are specific words**

| | |
|---|---|
| One | Wa7ad |
| Two | Tnen |
| Three | Tlete |
| Four | 2arb3a |
| Five | 5amse |
| Six | Sitte |
| Seven | Sab3a |
| Eight | Tmene |
| Nine | Tis3a |

**The tens are based on the root of the digit names, suffixed by *"een"*, except for <u>ten</u>**

| | |
|---|---|
| Ten | 3ashra |
| Twenty | 3ishreen |
| Thirty | Tleteen |
| Forty | 2arb3een |
| Fifty | 5amseen |
| Sixty | Sitteen |
| Seventy | Sab3een |
| Eighty | Tmeneen |
| Ninety | Tis3een |

**From eleven to nineteen, compound numbers are formed by stating the unit, then a form of the word for ten**

| | |
|---|---|
| Ten | 3ashra |
| Eleven | 7da3esh |
| Twelve | Tna3esh |
| Thirteen | Tlatta3esh |
| Fourteen | 2arba3ta3esh |
| Fifteen | 5amesta3esh |
| Sixteen | Sitta3esh |
| Seventeen | Sabe3ta3esh |
| Eighteen | Tmanta3esh |
| Nineteen | Tisi3ta3esh |

**Above twenty-one, compound numbers are formed by stating the unit then the ten, linked with the *and* word connector (*wa-*). Hence, we get:**

| | |
|---|---|
| Twenty | 3ishreen |
| Twenty-one | Wa7ad w 3ishreen |
| Twenty-two | Tnen w 3ishreen |
| Twenty-three | Tleta w 3ishreen |
| Twenty-four | 2arb3a w 3ishreen |
| Twenty-five | 5ams w 3ishreen |
| Twenty-six | Sitta w 3ishreen |
| Twenty-seven | Sab3a w 3ishreen |
| Twenty-eight | Tmena w 3ishreen |
| Twenty-nine | Tis3a w 3ishreen |
| Thirty | Tleteen |
| Forty | 2arb3een |

| | |
|---|---|
| Fifty | 5amseen |
| Sixty | Sitteen |
| Seventy | Sab3een |
| Eighty | Tmeneen |
| Ninety | Tis3een |

**Hundreds are formed by stating the multiplier digit before the word for hundred, except for <u>one hundred</u> itself**

| | |
|---|---|
| One Hundred | Miyye |
| One Hundred and one | Miyye w wa7ad |
| One Hundred and two | Miyye w tnen |
| One Hundred and thirty two | Miyye w tnena w tleteen |
| Two Hundred | Miten |
| Three Hundred | Tlat miyye |
| Four Hundred | 2arba3 miyye |
| Five Hundred | 5amis miyye |
| Six Hundred | Sit miyye |
| Seven Hundred | Sabe3 miyye |
| Eight Hundred | Tman miyye |
| Nine Hundred | Tisi3 miyye |

**The word for thousand is *2alef*. Two thousand is using the dual form of thousand: *2alfen***

| | |
|---|---|
| Thousand | 2alef |

**Above two thousand, the plural form of thousand is used**

| | |
|---|---|
| Two thousand | 2alfen |

| | |
|---|---|
| Three thousand | tlat talef |
| Four thousand | 2arba3 talef |
| Five thousand | 5ames talef |
| Six thousand | sit talef |
| Seven thousand | sabe3 talef |
| Eight thousand | tman talef |
| Nine thousand | tisi3 talef |

**The word for million is *malyon* and the word for billion is *milyar***

| | |
|---|---|
| Half | Nos |
| One-fourth | Rebe3 |
| One-third | Telet |

**When referring to an object**

| | |
|---|---|
| One car | Seyyara we7de |
| Two cars | Seyyarten |
| Three cars | Tlat seyyarat |
| Four cars | 2arba3 seyyarat |
| Five cars | 5ams seyyarat |
| Six cars | Sit seyyarat |
| Seven cars | Sabe3 seyyarat |
| Eight cars | Tman seyyarat |
| Nine cars | Tese3 seyyarat |
| Ten cars | 3asher seyyarat |
| Eleven cars | 7da3shar seyyara |
| Twelve cars | Tna3shar seyyara |
| Thirteen cars | Tlatta3shar seyyara |
| Fourteen cars | 2arba3ta3shar seyyara |
| Fifteen cars | 5amesta3shar seyyara |
| Twenty cars | 3ishreen seyyara |
| Twenty one cars | Wa7ad w 3ishreen seyyara |
| Thirty two cars | Tnena w tleteen seyyara |

## Test

**1. Write the number in Arabic:**

6:
13:
24:
37:
42:
56:
65:
71:
88:
93:
166:
241:
1999:
2019:

**2. Guess the numbers for the underlined words:**

Saba7 l 5er. Ana 2isme Marwan. Ne7na 5ayyen w 3ande tlat 2i5wet. Fi 3anna siyyarten. Ana 3ande tlat 3moom w 3amten. Fi 3ande kamen 2arba3 5wel w 5ames 5alet. Ne7na kelna sawa 3ashra bel 3ayle.

**5ayyen: Brothers**
**2i5wet: Sisters**
**Siyyarten: Cars**
**3moom: Uncles from father's side**
**3amten: Aunts from father's side**
**5wel: Uncles from Mother's side**
**5alet: Aunts from Mother's side**

## Answers

### 1. Write the number in Arabic:

6: Sitte
13: Tlatta3esh
24: 2arb3a w 3ishreen
37: Sab3a w tleteen
42: Tnen w 2arb3een
56: Sitta w 5amseen
65: 5amsa w sitteen
71: Wa7ad w sab3een
88: Tmena w tmeneen
93: Tleta w tis3een
166: Miyye w sitta w sitteen
241: Miten w wa7ad w 2arb3een
1999: 2alef w tese3miyye w tis3a w tis3een
2019: 2alfen w tese3ta3esh

### 2. Guess the numbers for the underlined words:

5ayyen: Tnen - 2
Tlat 2i5wet: Tlete - 3
Siyyarten: Tnen - 2
Tlat 3moom: Tlete - 3
3amten: Tnen - 2
2arba3 5wel: 2arb3a - 4
5ames 5alet: 5amse - 5
3ashra: 3ashra - 10

## Possessive Pronouns

Arabic uses pronoun suffixes as another way to indicate possession. In English we say "**my house**" "**his house**" etc. to indicate that something belongs to someone. In Arabic the same thing is done but the possessive pronouns are suffixed to the noun instead of written as independent words before the noun. Below is a chart of the possessive pronoun suffixes along with their corresponding independent pronouns.

| Independent Pronouns | Possessive Pronouns |
| --- | --- |
| Ana | ..e |
| Enta | ..ak |
| Ente | ..ik |
| Howwe | ..o |
| Hiyye | ..a |
| Ento | ..kon |
| Ne7na | ..na |
| Hinne | ..on |

When we attach pronoun suffixes to nouns, we are indicating who possesses the nouns and we are also making the nouns definite. For example, "his book" in Arabic is a combination of *Kteb* and the suffix *o*. When we combine them, we get *Ktebo*.

"your book" (masc.) is *Ktebak* and "their book" is *Ktebon*

|  | Possessive pronouns |
|---|---|
| My book | Kteb**e** |
| Your book | Kteb**ak** |
| Your book | Kteb**ik** |
| His book | Kteb**o** |
| Her book | Kteb**a** |
| Your book | Kteb**kon** |
| Our book | Kteb**na** |
| Their book | Kteb**on** |

**_Important:_** *the letter 't' shall be added before the possessive pronoun '..e' that refers to the subject pronoun 'I', when the respective noun ends with either an 'e' or an 'a' (feminine).*

Example:

Chair: Kirs**e**
My chair: Kirs**te**

That means, with the nouns ending with the stop sound (masculine), then the normal possessive pronoun '..e' shall be used. The nouns ending with 'a' or 'e' (feminine), then 't' shall be used before the possessive pronoun '..e'.

**Exercise:**

Please read the dialogue thoroughly and answer the following questions:

- Mar7aba. Ana 2isme Laila. Ana 3ande 2e5et w 5ay. Ana sekne b Beirut. Hayde 2oudte w hayde l 2ouda la 2i5wete.
- L bet fi 2arba3 2owad?
- Eh, l bet fi 2arba3 2owad. 2ooda we7de la ele. 2ouda we7de la 2i5wete. Hayde 2oudit ahle w salon.
- Ya3ne ento 5amse bel 3ayle?
- Eh, ne7na 5amse. 2aw2at byejo jidde w sitte, minseer sab3a bel bet.
- 2adde 3omron ahlik?
- Baba 3omro wa7da w 2arb3een w mama 3omra tis3a w tleteen. Hayde 2oudeton hon.
- Ok, tsharrafna Laila.
- Shokran, ana kamen

**Questions**

1. What is the girl's name?
2. How many brothers and sisters does she have?
3. Where does she live?
4. Does she have a room for herself, or is it shared with her siblings?
5. How many rooms does the house has?
6. What are the rooms in the house?
7. How many family members are they? How many with grandparents?
8. How old are her parents?

**Answers**

1. 2isma Laila. **Her name is Laila**
2. 3anda 2e5et w 5ay. **She has a sister and a brother**
3. Hiyye sekne b Beirut. **She lives in Beirut.**
4. Eh 3anda 2ouda la 7ala. **She has a room for herself**
5. L bet fi 2arba3 2owad. **The house has 4 rooms**
6. L bet fi 2ouda la Laila, 2ouda la 2i5weta, 2ouda la ahla w salon. **The house has a room for Laila, a room for her siblings, a room for her parents and a living room.**
7. Hinne 5amse. Sab3a ma3 jidda w sitta. **They are five family members. Seven with her grandpa and grandma.**
8. Bayya 3omro wa7da w 2arb3een w 2emma 3omra tis3a w tleteen. **Her father is 41 years old and her mother 39 years old.**

**Notes**

# Test

## Exercise 1:

### Table: ṫawle [f]

| | |
|---|---|
| My table | ……………….. |
| Your table (m) | ……………….. |
| Your table (f) | ……………….. |
| His table | ……………….. |
| Her table | ……………….. |
| Our table | ……………….. |
| Your table | ……………….. |
| Their table | ……………….. |

### tables: ṫawlet

| | |
|---|---|
| My tables | ……………….. |
| Your tables (m) | ……………….. |
| Your tables (f) | ……………….. |
| His tables | ……………….. |
| Her tables | ……………….. |
| Our tables | ……………….. |
| Your tables | ……………….. |
| Their tables | ……………….. |

*Hints and also to learn:*

| Book | My book | Pen | My pen | Pens | My pens |
|------|---------|-----|--------|------|---------|
| Kteb | Ktebe | Alam | Alame | 2lem | 2leme |

| Ball | My ball | Fork | My fork | Forks | My forks |
|------|---------|------|---------|-------|----------|
| Ṫabe [f] | Ṫabte | Shawke[f] | Shawkte | Shiwak[f] | Shiwake |

## Exercise 2:

1. Their pens: ………………

2. Our balls: ………………

3. Your(pl) fork: ……………..

4. His table: ………………

5. Her cup: ………………

## Answers

## Exercise 1:

**Table: tawle [f]**

Tawelte
Taweltak
Taweltik
Tawelto
Tawelta
Tawletna (e is short)
Tawletkon (e is short)
Tawleton (e is short)

**tables: tawlet**

Tawletna
Tawletak
Tawletik
Tawleto
Tawleta
Tawletna (e is long)
Tawletkon (e is long)
Tawleton (e is long)

## Exercise 2:

1.2lemna – 2.Tabetna – 3.Shawkitkon – 4.Tawelto – 5.Finjena

# Extra material

*Grammar, Possessive Phrases:*

1. For masculine nouns we use the object followed by the noun.

2. For feminine nouns ending with vowels we use the object+it followed by the noun.

3. For phrases with names we use the object followed by definitive noun.

| | |
|---|---|
| Elie's book | Kteb Elie |
| Sandra's flowers | Wrood Sandra |
| Beirut River | Naher Beirut |
| Layla's and Ali's tree | Shajrit Layla w Ali |
| Ali's and Sandra's books | Kotob Ali w Sandra |
| This is Dani's fork | Hayde shawkit Dani |
| These are Aya's books | Hole kotob Aya |
| The boy's book | Kteb l sabe |
| The girl's flowers | Wrood l benet |
| The house's window | Shibbek l bet |
| The kitchen's door | Beb l matba5 |
| The mother's chair | Kirse l em |
| Her fork and knife | Shawketa w sekkinta |
| My mother and father | Emme w bayye |

## Time-Telling

**How to ask for time in Arabic?**

We are going to learn how to tell the time to the hour and minute in Arabic.

If you would like to ask someone for the time in Arabic, you should say:

*2adde l se3a*, which means: how much is the time?

The answer is:

*L se3a...*: The time is...

| O'clock | L se3a |
|---|---|
| One O'clock | L se3a we7de |
| Two O'clock | L se3a tinten |
| Three O'clock | L se3a tlete |
| Four O'clock | L se3a 2arb3a |
| Five O'clock | L se3a 5amse |
| Six O'clock | L se3a sitte |
| Seven O'clock | L se3a sab3a |
| Eight O'clock | L se3a tmene |
| Nine O'clock | L se3a tis3a |
| Ten O'clock | L se3a 3ashra |
| Eleven O'clock | L se3a 7da3esh |
| Twelve O'clock | L se3a tna3esh |

To say 'past' in Arabic, we use '**w**' which comes after the hour (which is also 'and'), so half past two in Arabic would literally be 'two o'clock and a half': ***L se3a tinten w nos.***

| Past | W |
|---|---|
| Five past | W 5amse |
| Ten past | W 3ashra |
| Quarter past | W rebe3 |
| Twenty past | W telet |
| Half past | W nos |

To say **'to'** in Arabic, we use **'2ella'** which comes after the hour, so 'quarter to three' in Arabic would literally be **'three o'clock less a quarter'**: *Tlete 2ella rebe3*

| To | 2ella |
|---|---|
| Five to | 2ella 5amse |
| Ten to | 2ella 3ashra |
| Quarter to | 2ella rebe3 |
| Twenty to | 2ella telet |

**Notes**

## Test

**Exercise 1:**

What time is it? *Adde l se3a?*

It is one o'clock:  *L se3a we7de*

It is five o'clock:

It is 10:30:

It is 10:25:

It is 4:35:

It is 3:45:

It is 8:50:

It is 11:15:

It is 9:20:

It is 7:40:

## Exercise 2:

What time is it? *Adde l se3a?*

# Answers:

## Exercise 1:

It is five o'clock: *L se3a 5amse*

It is 10:30: *L se3a 3ashra w nos*

It is 10:25: *L se3a 3ashra w nos ella 5amse*

It is 4:35: *L se3a 2arb3a w nos w 5amse*

It is 3:45: *L se3a 2arb3a 2ella rebe3*

It is 8:50: *L se3a tis3a 2ella 3ashra*

It is 11:15: *L se3a 7da3esh w rebe3*

It is 9:20: *L se3a tis3a w telet*

It is 7:40: *L se3a tmene ella telet*

## Exercise 2:

| L se3a sab3a w nos | L se3a 3ashra w nos | L se3a tis3a w nos |
|---|---|---|

| L se3a tna3esh ella telet | L se3a tlete ella 3ashra | L se3a tis3a w 5amse |
|---|---|---|

| L se3a tlete w nos w 5amse | L se3a tna3esh ella telet | L se3a tna3esh w telet |
|---|---|---|

A minute: d2i2a
A second: senye
An hour/ a watch: se3a

Minutes: da2ayi2
Seconds: sawene
Hours: se3at

| Minute (Eng) | Minute(s) (Ar) | Hour(s) (Ar) | Day(s) (Ar) |
|---|---|---|---|
| 1 | D2i2a | Se3a | Yom |
| 2 | D2i2ten | Se3ten | Yawmen |
| 3 | Tlat d2ayi2 | Tlat se3at | Tlat tiyyem |
| 4 | 2arba3 d2ayi2 | 2arba3 se3at | 2arba3 tiyyem |
| 5 | 5ams d2ayi2 | 5ams se3at | 5ams tiyyem |
| 6 | Sit d2ayi2 | Sit se3at | Sit tiyyem |
| 7 | Sab3 d2ayi2 | Sabe3 se3at | Sabe3 tiyyem |
| 8 | Tman d2ayi2 | Tman se3at | Tman tiyyem |
| 9 | Tis3 d2ayi2 | Tis3 se3at | Tis3 tiyyem |
| 10 | 3ashr d2ayi2 | 3asher se3at | 3asher tiyyem |
| 11 | 7da3shar d2i2a | 7da3shar se3a | 7da3shar yom |
| 12 | Tna3shar d2i2a | Tna3shar se3a | Tna3shar yom |
| 13 | Tlatta3shar d2i2a | Tlatta3shar se3a | Tlatta3shar yom |
| 14 | 2arba3ta3shar d2i2a | 2arba3ta3shar se3a | 2arba3ta3shar yom |
| 15 | 5amesta3shar d2i2a | 5amesta3shar se3a | 5amesta3shar yom |
| 16 | Sitta3shar d2i2a | Sitta3shar se3a | Sitta3shar yom |
| 17 | Sabe3ta3shar d2i2a | Sabe3ta3shar se3a | Sabe3ta3shar yom |
| 18 | Tmanta3shar d2i2a | Tmanta3shar se3a | Tmanta3shar yom |
| 19 | Tisi3ta3shar d2i2a | Tisi3ta3shar se3a | Tisi3ta3shar yom |
| 20 | 3ishreen d2i2a | 3ishreen se3a | 3ishreen yom |
| 100 | Meet d2i2a | Meet se3a | Meet yom |
| 101 | Miyye w d2i2a | Miyye w se3a | Miyye w yom |
| 102 | Miyye w d2i2ten | Miyye w se3ten | Miyye w yawmen |

| 1000 | Alef d2i2a | Alef se3a | Alef yom |
| 1001 | Alef w d2i2a | Alef w se3a | Alef w yom |

## Colors

| Color | Colors in Arabic | Feminine | Masculine | Plural |
|---|---|---|---|---|
| Black | 2aswad | Sawda | 2aswad | Sood |
| White | 2abyad | Bayda | 2abyad | Beed |
| Red | 2a7mar | 7amra | 2a7mar | 7omor |
| Green | 2a5dar | 5adra | 2a5dar | 5odor |
| Blue | 2azra2 | Zar2a | 2azra2 | Zere2 |
| Yellow | 2asfar | Safra | 2asfar | Sofor |
| Grey | Rmede | Rmediyye | Rmede | Rmede |

The masculine forms of the colors above have the same pattern as regular adjectives.

| I bought a red car | Shtaret sayara 7amra |
|---|---|
| His house is green | Bayto 2a5dar |
| We all live in a yellow submarine | Kelna 3ayshin b ghawwasa safra |

Arabic also has nouns for colors equivalent to English terms such as "blueness," "greenness," and "blackness." These words are listed below.

| English | Arabic |
|---|---|
| Blackness | Sawed |
| Whiteness | Bayad |
| Redness | 7amaar |
| Greenness | 5adaar |
| Blueness | Zaraa2 |
| Yellowness | Safaar |

For comparative reasons, we add the word 'aktar' after the adjective. **Aktar** means **more**.

| The water in Beirut is bluer than in Germany | L may b Beirut zar2a aktar min l may b 2ilmanya |
|---|---|
| The pen is redder than the paper | L 2alam 2a7mar aktar min l war2a |

**Exercise:**

Please read the following text thoroughly and the answer the questions:

- Ayya se3a jeet lyom 3al bet?
- Ana b5allis madrase 3al se3a tinten w nos. Bousal 3al bet 3al se3a tlete 2ella rebe3.
- Sho bta3mil bas tousal 3al bet?
- Bil3ab b le3ebte l 7amra.
- W hayde l li3be l bayda la meen?
- Hayde le3bit 5ayye. Fi 3ando le3be 7amra kamen bas ana le3ebte 7amra aktar min le3ebto.

**Questions**

1. What time does he finish school?
2. What time does he usually arrive home?
3. What does he do when he comes home?
4. What color does his toy have?
5. For whom is the other toy and what color does it have?
6. What toy is redder, his or his brothers?

## Answers

1. Howwe bi5allis madrase 3al se3a tinten w nos. *He finishes school at 2:30.*
2. Byousal 3al bet 3al se3a tlete 2ella rebe3. *He arrives home at 2:45.*
3. Byil3ab b le3ebto. *He plays with his toy*
4. Le3ebto 7amra. *His toy is red*
5. L li3be l tenye la 5ayyo w lon l le3be abyad. *The other toy is for his brother and it's a white one.*
6. Le3ebto 7amra aktar min 5ayo. *His toy is redder than his brothers.*

## Notes

# Days and Months

Days of the week are essential vocabularies in any language and Arabic isn't an exception. List of days of the week in Arabic with pronounce and English translations.

| English | Arabic |
|---|---|
| Monday | Tanen |
| Tuesday | Taleta |
| Wednesday | 2orb3a |
| Thursday | 5amees |
| Friday | Jom3a |
| Saturday | Sabet |
| Sunday | 2a7ad |

How to tell days of the week in Arabic in past tense:

By adding the word "**L maade**" which means "the last" after the day.

| The last | L maade |
|---|---|

So, it will become:

| English | Lebanese Arabic |
|---|---|
| Last Monday | L tanen l maade |
| Last Tuesday | L taleta l maade |
| Last Wednesday | L 2orb3a l maade |
| Last Thursday | L 5amees l maade |
| Last Friday | L jom3a l maade |
| Last Saturday | L sabet l maade |
| Last Sunday | L 2a7ad l maade |

How to tell days of the week in Arabic in future tense:

By adding the word "**L jeye**" which means "**the upcoming**" after the day

So, it will be:

| The upcoming | L jeye |
|---|---|

| English | Lebanese Arabic |
|---|---|
| Upcoming Monday | L tanen l jeye |
| Upcoming Tuesday | L taleta l jeye |
| Upcoming Wednesday | L 2orb3a l jeye |
| Upcoming Thursday | L 5amees l jeye |
| Upcoming Friday | L jom3a l jeye |
| Upcoming Saturday | L sabet l jeye |
| Upcoming Sunday | L 2a7ad l jeye |

The list below are the months of the year that are used in the Lebanese Arabic:

| No. | Month | Arabic Name |
|---|---|---|
| 1 | January | Kenoon l tene |
| 2 | February | Shbat |
| 3 | March | 2azaar |
| 4 | April | Neesen |
| 5 | May | 2ayyar |
| 6 | June | 7zayran |
| 7 | July | Tamooz |
| 8 | August | 2aab |
| 9 | September | 2aylool |
| 10 | October | Tishreen l 2awwal |
| 11 | November | Tishreen l tene |
| 12 | December | Kenoon l awwal |

**Info:**

| **Seasons of the year** | **Fsool l sine** |
|---|---|
| Autumn | 5areef |
| Winter | Sheta |
| Spring | Rabee3 |
| Summer | Sef |
| Which season do you[m] like? | Ayya fasil bit7ib? |

## Test

**Exercise 1:**

Please translate the following text:

L tanen l made re7na shtarayna seyyara sawda. L 5amees l jeye, ra7 na3mela bayda. Ne7na jebna seyyara b 2ayyar 2alfen w 7da3esh, bas ntaza3it b kenoon l tene 2alfen w 2arba3ta3esh. Lyom 3al se3a tna3esh w nos ra7 njeeb l seyyara.

**Exercise 2:**

| | |
|---|---|
| What day is today? | Shu lyom?/ Lyom Shu? |
| Today is Wednesday | Lyom l Orb3a |
| **What is tomorrow?** | ……………………….................... |
| **What was yesterday?** | ……………………….................... |

What date is it?          Adde l teree5?
04 August 2011     2arb3a 2aab 2alfen w 7da3esh

**What is tomorrow's date?** ……………………………….......

## Answers

### Exercise 1:

Last Monday we went and bought a black car. Next Thursday, we will do it white. We brought a car in May 2011, but it broke in January 2014. Today at 12:30 we will go and get the car.

### Exercise 2:

**What is tomorrow?** Bokra l 5amees

**What was yesterday?** Mberi7 ken l taleta

**What is tomorrow's date?** 5amse 2aab 2alfen w 7da3esh

## Verb Conjugations

I think it's time to dive again in the grammar, right?

In this chapter we're going to be talking about verb conjugations.

The base form is the most basic form of a verb, free of any prefixes or suffixes.

In both Arabic and English, the base form is the form of a verb listed in dictionary entries. In English, this is the infinitive (**be, go, have, etc…**).

In Arabic, the base form is the **third-person masculine singular** (**howwe**) of the perfect tense. So, although the verb "ra7", for example, might literally mean 'he went' in a sentence, when cited in isolation, its translation would be *'go'* or *'to go'*, the infinitive.

Let's start with the Present, present continuous and in one case, the active participle.

**Nem: to sleep**

| Subject Pronouns English | Subject Pronouns Arabic | Present | Present Continuous |
|---|---|---|---|
| I | Ana | Bnem | 3am nem |
| You (m) | Enta | Bitnem | 3am tnem |
| You (f) | Ente | Bitneme | 3am tneme |
| He | Howwe | Binem | 3am ynem |
| She | Hiyye | Bitnem | 3am tnem |
| You (pl) | Ento | Bitnemo | 3am tnemo |
| We | Ne7na | Minnem | 3am nnem |
| They | Hinne | Binemo | 3am ynemo |

If you want to express a habitual meaning (that you do something regularly), you have to use the present tense. And if you want to express a present continuous meaning (that you "are doing" something right now), you often use present continuous tense, although sometimes you must use the active participle instead.

The present and present continuous are negated by adding the prefix "**Ma**" before the verb.

I am falling asleep: ***Ana 3am nem.*** *(action done, yet still going)*
I don't sleep: ***Ana ma bnem.***
I am not sleeping: ***Ana ma 3am nem.***

| Subject Pronouns English | Subject Pronouns Arabic | Present | Active Participle |
|---|---|---|---|
| I | Ana | Bnem | Neyim |
| You (m) | Enta | Bitnem | Neyim |
| You (f) | Ente | Bitneme | Neyme |
| He | Howwe | Binem | Neyim |
| She | Hiyye | Bitnem | Neyme |
| You (pl) | Ento | Bitnemo | Neymin |
| We | Ne7na | Minnem | Neymin |
| They | Hinne | Binemo | Neymin |

The present tense is negated by adding the prefix "**Ma**" before the verb. However, the active participle is negated by adding the prefix "**manne**" before the verb.

I am asleep: **Ana neyim.**
I don't sleep: **Ana ma bnem.**
I am not asleep: **Ana manne neyim.**

## Lebis: to wear

| Subject Pronouns English | Subject Pronouns Arabic | Present | Present Continuous |
|---|---|---|---|
| I | Ana | Bilbos | 3am bilbos |
| You (m) | Enta | Btilbos | 3am tilbos |
| You (f) | Ente | Btelebse | 3am telebse |
| He | Howwe | Byilbos | 3am yilbos |
| She | Hiyye | Btilbos | 3am tilbos |
| You (pl) | Ento | Btelebso | 3am telebso |
| We | Ne7na | Mnilbos | 3am nilbos |
| They | Hinne | Byelebso | 3am yelebso |

| Subject Pronouns English | Subject Pronouns Arabic | Present | Active Participle |
|---|---|---|---|
| I | Ana | Bilbos | Lebis |
| You (m) | Enta | Btilbos | Lebis |
| You (f) | Ente | Btelebse | Lebse |
| He | Howwe | Byilbos | Lebis |
| She | Hiyye | Btilbos | Lebse |
| You (pl) | Ento | Btelebso | Lebsin |
| We | Ne7na | Mnilbos | Lebsin |
| They | Hinne | Byelebso | Lebsin |

I wear: **Ana bilbos**
I am wearing (Doing the action): **Ana 3am bilbos**
I am wearing (At this moment): **Ana lebis**

**Ekol: to eat**

| Subject Pronouns English | Subject Pronouns Arabic | Present | Present Continuous |
|---|---|---|---|
| I | Ana | Bekol | 3am bekol |
| You (m) | Enta | Btekol | 3am tekol |
| You (f) | Ente | Btekle | 3am tekle |
| He | Howwe | Byekol | 3am yekol |
| She | Hiyye | Btekol | 3am tekol |
| You (pl) | Ento | Bteklo | 3am teklo |
| We | Ne7na | Mnekol | 3am nekol |
| They | Hinne | Byeklo | 3am yeklo |

Here there is no need for the active participle.

**Example:**

Yalla jehzin?
*Are you ready?*

Eh, yalla hayyena lebsin w jehzin
*Yes, we are dressed and ready*

La2 la7za, ana manne lebis, hayyene 3am bekol
*No wait, I am not dressed, I am eating*

Le 3am tekol? Badna nroo7 3ala mat3am
*Why are you eating? We want to go to a restaurant*

Eh ma bi2assir. Ana 3atool jo3an!
*It's alright. I am always hungry!*

**Notes**

## Past Tense

For the appropriate verb conjugations, see the past tense (L maade) conjugations here. **Usage of the past tense in the Lebanese Arabic is fairly simple; you use it as much as you would in English.**

| Subject Pronouns English | Subject Pronouns Arabic | Present | Past |
|---|---|---|---|
| I | Ana | Bnem | Nemet |
| You (m) | Enta | Bitnem | Nemet |
| You (f) | Ente | Bitneme | Nimte |
| He | Howwe | Binem | Nem |
| She | Hiyye | Bitnem | Nemit |
| You (pl) | Ento | Bitnemo | Nemto |
| We | Ne7na | Minnem | Nemna |
| They | Hinne | Binemo | Nemo |

| Subject Pronouns English | Subject Pronouns Arabic | Present | Past |
|---|---|---|---|
| I | Ana | Bilbos | Lbeset |
| You (m) | Enta | Btilbos | Lbeset |
| You (f) | Ente | Btelebse | Lbiste |
| He | Howwe | Byilbos | Lebes |
| She | Hiyye | Btilbos | Lebset |
| You (pl) | Ento | Btelebso | Lbesto |
| We | Ne7na | Mnilbos | Lbisna |
| They | Hinne | Byelebso | Lebso |

**The past tense is negated by adding the prefix "Ma" before the verb.**

I didn't wear: *Ana ma Ibeset.*

**Example:**

Ana nemet mberi7 shi 3asher se3at!
*Yesterday I slept for about 10 hours!*

Ouf! Ana nemet bas 5ames se3at! Kenet kel l lel 3am fakkir
*Ouf! I slept only 5 hours! The whole night I was thinking*

B sho kenet 3am tfakkir?
*What were you thinking about?*

Tzakkaret lamma kenna zghar w kenna nil3ab sawa bel jnayne.
*I remembered when we were little and we used to play together in the garden.*

Kenit 2iyyem 7ilwe. Marra lbesna ana weyyek nafes l tyeb.
*Good old days. We once wore the same clothes.*

Eh, kina nilbos t-shirtet 3layon Mickey Mouse.
*Yes, we used to wear T-shirts that had Mickey Mouse on them.*

**Notes**

_____
_____
_____
_____
_____
_____
_____
_____
_____
_____

## The Imperfect Tense

**Form:**

While the perfect tense is conjugated using suffixes, the imperfect tense uses prefixes.

The imperfect prefixes and suffixes are not added to the base form but an imperfect stem.

**Use:**

- The imperfect can follow an auxiliary. An auxiliary can be an active participle, conjugated - verb, or other certain types of words. The equivalent in English is modal verbs and others that can precede a second verb (which is infinitive or gerund). For example, can go, want to eat, like dancing. In these examples, can, want, and like function as auxiliaries.
- The imperfect is also used to express the future when preceded by the particle "ra7" or the prefixed particle "7a".
- The imperfect follows the progressive particle "3am", equivalent to the present continuous tense of English. It refers to actions happening at the time of speaking, as well as those that are repetitive or ongoing.
- A negative imperative is expressed by placing "ma" in front of a second-person imperfect verb.
- An imperfect verb follows certain conjunctions of purpose and time

It can also be combined with the verb "**Ken**" which means "**I used to...**" or to refer to an action that was taking place in the past. *(ex. was doing)*

Example: I used to write: **Ana kenet 2ektob**

However, the verb "**ken**" also changes according to the pronoun.

| Pronouns | Used to: Ken | To write: 2ektob |
|---|---|---|
| Ana | Kenet | 2ektob |
| Enta | Kenet | Tektob |
| Ente | Kente | Teketbe |
| Howwe | Ken | Yiktob |
| Hiyye | Kenit | Tiktob |
| Ento | Kento | Teketbo |
| Ne7na | Kenna | Niktob |
| Hinne | Keno | Yeketbo |

# The Bi-Imperfect

**Form:**

The Bi-Imperfect is formed by prefixing 'b' to conjugations in the imperfect tense.

**Use:**

- The Bi-Imperfect tense most often corresponds to the present simple tense of English, referring to general truths and habits.
- The Bi-imperfect can also refer to future, especially to convey intentions.
- The progressive article '3am' is usually followed by a bare imperfect verb, but can, less commonly, precede a Bi-imperfect verb.
- The Bi-imperfect is sometimes interchangeable with the imperfect. Their uses may vary among native speakers, not only from region to region but within the same region, as well.

**Daras: to study**

| Pronouns | Prefix | Verb: Study Daras |
|---|---|---|
| Ana | Bi- | Bidros |
| Enta | Bti- | Btidros |
| Ente | Bte- | Btederse |
| Howwe | Bi | Biedros/Byedros |
| Hiyye | Bti- | Btidros |
| Ento | Bte---o | Btederso |
| Ne7na | Mni- | Mnidros |
| Hinne | Bye---o | Byederso |

I study: **Ana bidros** (means I usually study. Might refer to school or learning a new language for instance)

Example:

- Ente bel jem3a? *(Are you in the university?)*
- Eh, ana bidros biology.
- W 5ayyik sho byidros?
- 5ayye byidros physics w 2i5te btidros timseel. *(acting)*

## Future Tense

Want to tell the Future? Here's how – Using "Ra7" in Lebanese Arabic.

As with any other language, Lebanese Arabic has a future tense, however it differs slightly from that of Fus-ha.

While Fus-ha uses "sa" or "sawfa" to indicate something that will happen in the future, Lebanese Arabic uses the word "ra7".

It is combined with the imperfect tense.

Let's look at some examples to make this perfectly clear:

| English | Lebanese Arabic |
|---|---|
| I will read the book | Ana ra7 2e2ra l kteb |
| I will buy ice cream | Ana ra7 2ishtre bouza |

There is no need to conjugate "ra7" according to the pronoun. Have a look at the table below using the word *yishrab* (to drink).

| Pronoun | English | Lebanese |
|---------|---------|----------|
| I | I will drink | Ana ra7 2ishrab |
| You (m) | You will drink | Enta ra7 tishrab |
| You (f) | You will drink | Ente ra7 tishrabe |
| He | He will drink | Howwe ra7 yishrab |
| She | She will drink | Hiyye ra7 tishrab |
| You (Pl.) | You will drink | Ento ra7 tishrabo |
| We | We will drink | Ne7na ra7 nishrab |
| They | They will drink | Hinne ra7 yishrabo |

**Example:**

- Ana ra7 roo7 3al dikkene. Badkon shi?
  *I am going to the market. You need anything?*
- Eh, feek tjible 3ilbit do5an?
  *Yes, can you bring me a pack of cigarettes?*
- Meshe, ra7 jeeb 3ilbit do5an. Fi shi tene?
  *Alright, I'll get a pack of cigarettes. Anything else?*
- Badna batata, bas ne7na ba3den ra7 minroo7 njib.
  *We need potatoes, bas we will go later to get some.*

## Comparative/Superlative

In Arabic, superlative and comparative constructions are expressed using the form *2af3al*. We need to mould adjectives using the *2af3al* form as follow:

Sahel (easy) – 2ashal (easier)
Sa3eb (hard) – 2as3ab (harder)
7elo (Pretty) – 2a7la (prettier)
Kbeer (big) – 2akbar (bigger)

When we use the *2af3al* form followed by a noun, we make a superlative construction, e.g.

The largest building= 2akbar bineye
The prettiest girl= 2a7la benet
The oldest book= 2a2dam kteb
The easiest exam= 2ashal 2emti7an

When we use the *2af3al* form followed by the preposition *min*, we make a comparative construction, e.g.

Ali is shorter than Hassan= Ali 2a2sar <u>min</u> Hassan
A city is larger than a village= L madeene 2akbar <u>min</u> l day3a
My room is smaller than yours= 2oudte 2azghar <u>min</u> 2oudtak

## Test

Translate the following sentences:

Arabic is the hardest language I studied:
-----------------------------------------

I am taller than my sister:
-----------------------------------------

New York is bigger than Beirut:
-----------------------------------------

I live on the longest street in the city:
-----------------------------------------

## Answers

**Arabic is the hardest language I studied:** L 3arabe/ L logha l 3arabiyye hiyye 2as3ab logha darasta

**I am taller than my sister:** Ana 2atwal min 2i5te

**New York is bigger than Beirut:** New York 2akbar min Beirut

**I live on the longest street in the city:** ana 3ayesh b 2atwal sheri3 bel madeene

## Compound Tenses

Compound tenses are created by following **ken 'to be'** with a perfect or imperfect verb or active participle. The most common combinations are shown in the table below, using the verb **3imil** **'to do'** as an example.

| Perfect verb | Ken 3imil | He had done |
|---|---|---|
| Imperfect verb | Ken ya3mil | He used to do |
| Continuous particle | Ken 3am ya3mil | He was doing |
| Future particle | Ken rah ya3mil | He was going to do |
| Active participle | Ken 3amil | He was doing |

# Clothing

As mentioned before, nouns in Arabic (Lebanese Arabic) can be either Masculine or Feminine. Sadly, this makes everything a bit more complicated. However, I have included in the table down below some nouns of clothing that you can try and know by heart.

| English | Masculine | Feminine | Dual | Plural |
|---|---|---|---|---|
| Shirt | 2amees | | 2ameesen | 2imsan |
| T-shirt | | T-shirt | T-shirten | T-shirtet |
| Pants | Bantalon | | Bantalonen | Bnatleen |
| Shoes | Sobbat | | Sobbaten | Sbabeet |
| Heels | | Skarbeene | Skarbeenten | Skarbeenet |
| Dress | Fostan | | Fostanen | Fsateen |
| Skirt | | Tannoura | Tannourten | Tneneer |
| Short | Short | | Shorten | Shortet |
| Slippers/Flip-flops | Mishheye | | Mishheyten | Mishheyet |
| Socks | | | Kalseten | Kalset |
| Suit | | Badle | Badelten | Badlet |
| Jeans | Jeans/Jeenz | | Jeansen | Jeenzet |
| Scarf | Shel | | Shelen | Shelet |
| Sandals | Sandal | | Sandalen | Sanadeel |

Ofcourse you're going to be needing adjectives for describing your clothes. I know I do, especially over the holidays where I need to say:
*Badde Jeans akbar*

The adjective also followed the gender of the noun. If a noun is masculine, you have to include a masculine adjective. The same thing goes to Feminine and Plural.

| Characteristics | Masculine | Feminine | Plural |
| --- | --- | --- | --- |
| Long/tall | Taweel | Taweele | Twal |
| Short | 2aseer | 2aseera | 2saar |
| Large/wide | 3areed | 3areeda | 3raad |
| Small/young | Zgheer | Zgheere | Zghar |
| Big/old | Kbeer | Kbeere | Kbar |
| Narrow/tight | Dayyi2 | Day2a | Day2een |
| Beautiful | 7elo | 7ilwe | 7ilwin |
| Ugly | Bishi3 | Bish3a | Bish3een |

Example:
I want a short skirt: Badde Tannoura 2aseera
I want a a large shirt: Badde 2amees 3areed

## Exercise:

A red shirt　　　The red shirt　　　The shirt is red
..........................　..........................　..........................

Give me a red shirt　Hand us yellow shorts　Give us a tight suit
..........................　..........................　..........................

I want black shoes　We want pink skirts　These sandals are small
..........................　..........................　..........................

Hand us the blue dress　Hand me a small white shirt　Give me golden socks
..........................　..........................　..........................

The blue shirt is wide　This white shirt is small　The pink socks are beautiful
..........................　..........................　..........................

Is the red dress beautiful?　This shirt is ugly　I want a red car
..........................　..........................　..........................

## Answers

A red shirt　　　The red shirt　　　The shirt is red
Kanze 7amra　　L Kanze l 7amra　　L kanze 7amra

Give me a red shirt　Hand us yellow shorts　Give us a tight suit
3tine kanze 7amra　3tina shortat sofor　3tina badle day2a

I want black shoes　We want pink skirts　These sandals are small
bade sobbat 2aswad　badna tnenir zaher　hole l sanadel zghar

Hand us the blue dress　Hand me a small white shirt　Give me golden socks
3tina l fostan l 2azra2　3tine kanze zgheere bayda　3tine kalset dahabiyye

The blue shirt is wide　　This white shirt is small
L kanze l zar2a wes3a　　Hayde l kanze l bayda zgheere

The pink socks are beautiful
L kalset l zaher 7ilwin

Is the red dress beautiful?　This shirt is ugly　I want a red car
7elo l fostan l 2a7mar?　Hayde l kanze l bish3a　Badde seyyara 7amra

# Professions

Let's start with how you can ask people what do they do.

| English | Masculine | Feminine |
|---|---|---|
| What do you do? | Sho bta3mil? | Sho bta3emle? |
| What do you work? | Sho btishteghel? | Sho btishteghle? |

Here are some professions, that you could use while visiting/living in Lebanon:

| English | Masculine | Feminine |
|---|---|---|
| Doctor | 7akeem | 7akeeme |
| Engineer | Mhandis | Mhandse |
| Teacher | 2istez | M3alme |
| Lawyer | Mo7ame | Mo7amiyye |
| Writer | Ketib | Ketbe |
| Jeweler | Jawharje | Jawharjiyye |
| Baker | 5abbez | 5abbeze |
| Actor | Momassil | Momassile |
| Politician | Siyese | Siyesiyye |
| Carpenter | Najjar | Najjara |
| Blacksmith | 7added | 7addede |
| Nurse | Nurse | Nurse |
| Manager | Manager/Mas2ool | Manager/Mas2oole |
| Employee | Mwazzaf | mwazzafe |

## Info to use in the upcoming test

| | |
|---|---|
| Ana mhandis | I am an engineer. |
| Inta/Inte sho? | What is your job? (what are you?) |
| What do you do? | Sho bta3mil? [m] Sho bta3imle? [f] |
| What do you work? | Sho btishtighil? [m] sho btishtighle? [f] |
| Ana 7akeem. | I am a doctor. |

## Test

Answer the following questions:

1. Hayde ketbe?
Eh, _____ .

2. Hayda 7added?
La2, _____ .

3. Sho hayda?
_____ .

4. Sho hayde?
_____ .

5. Hayde Siyesiyye?
_____ .

6. Hayde ketbe?
_____ .

**Answers:**

1. *Hayde ketbe*
2. *Hayda 7akeem*
3. *Hayda 2istez*
4. *Hayde mhandse*
5. *La2, hayda siyese*
6. *Eh, hayde ketbe*

**Grammar**

**Simple Phrases**

Noun + Defined noun --- Doctor + The Family = doctor of the family

The Family Doctor **7akeem l 3ayle**

Now, the whole phrase is defined, which means The Family Doctor = The Family Doctor is

**Example: The Family Doctor is good = 7akeem l 3ayle mni7**

Note: For feminine nouns that end with a vowel we use the object+it followed by the noun

Female doctor is **7akeeme**

Example: The Family (female)Doctor is good = **7akeemit l 3ayle mni7a**

# The Human Body

We can all say that Beirut is a really big city. Let's say it's summer and there's some construction going on. We should be honest to ourselves and say that it might happen that you get a headache when you're there. But how can you say that you have a headache? Don't worry, I am here for you.

I have included some biology stuff in this book. Check out the table down below.

| English | Masculine | Feminine | Dual | Plural |
|---|---|---|---|---|
| Head | Ras | | Rasen | Roos |
| Eye | | 3en | 3aynten | 3yoon |
| Eyebrow | 7ajib | | 7ajben | 7wejib |
| Nose | Min5ar | | Min5aren | Mne5eer |
| Ear | | Dayne | Daynten | Dinen |
| Neck | | Ra2be | Ra2ebten | R2aab |
| Hair | | | | Sha3er |
| A Hair | | Sha3ra | Sha3irten | Sha3er |
| Leg | 2ijir | | 2ijirten | 2ijren |
| Foot | 2ijir | | 2ijirten | 2ijren |
| Knee | | Rikbe | Rikibten | Rkaab |
| Chest | Seder | | Sidren | Sdoora |
| Back | Daher | | Dahren | Dhoor |
| Shoulder | Kitif | | Kitfen | Ktef |
| Hand | | 2eed | 2eedten | 2eeden |
| Arm | | 2eed | 2eedten | 2eeden |
| Elbow | Koo3 | | Koo3en | Kwe3 |
| Hand Palm | Kaff | | Kaffen | Kfoof |
| Finger | 2osba3 | | 2osba3en | 2sabee3 |

I know. I know. These are just the nouns and 'headache' is nowhere to be seen.

Ache has the same meaning as pain and the translation of them would be: *Waja3*.

**I have pain: *Ana 3ande waja3.***

When you say I have a headache, you're surely referring to your own head. That's why we have to add the possessive pronoun '-e' to the noun.

Hence,

I have a headache: *Ras<u>e</u> 3am youja3ne.*

My shoulder hurts: *Kitf<u>e</u> 3am youja3ne.*

His shoulder hurts: *Kitf<u>o</u> 3am youja3o.*

**Exercise:**

I have a mouth          I have a red mouth     My mouth is red
..............................    ....................................    ..................................

He has black hair    Does she have brown hair?   We have long legs
..............................    ....................................    ..................................

My eyes are blue    I have two elbows    We have five fingers
..............................    ....................................    ..................................

She has big head    He has a small nose    You have beautiful hair
..............................    ....................................    ..................................

## Answers:

I have a mouth    I have a red mouth    My mouth is red
   3ande tim        3ande tim 2a7mar      timme 2a7mar

He has black hair    DFoes she have brown hair?    We have long legs
3ando sha3er 2aswad    3anda sha3er binne?    3anna 2ijren twal

My eyes are blue    I have two elbows    We have five fingers
   3yoone zere2       3ande koo3en       3anna 2asabi3

She has big head    He has a small nose    You have beautiful hair

3anda ras kbir      3ando min5ar zgheer     3andik/3andak sha3er 7elo

# Relatives

Relatives... You either love them or hate them. Family in the Lebanese culture is really important. You always have to call your grandma or your aunt over the holidays to congratulate her for holiday, although she is not the one that made up the holiday. But it doesn't matter, you just have to. It's the rules.

In the table down below, you will find the translation of every relative there is, including when you want to say that it's your own relative.

| English | Lebanese Arabic | My... |
| --- | --- | --- |
| Father | Bay | Bayye |
| Mother | Imm | Imme |
| Brother | 5ay | 5ayye |
| Sister | 2i5it | 2i5te |
| Son | 2eben | 2ebne |
| Daughter | Binit | Binte |
| Grandfather | Jidd | Jidde |
| Grandmother | Sitt | Sitte |
| Uncle (Father side) | 3am | 3amme |
| Uncle (mother side) | 5al | 5ale |
| Aunt (father side) | 3amme | 3amte |
| Aunt (mother side) | 5ale | 5alte |
| Grandson | 7afeed | 7afeede |
| Granddaughter | 7afeede | 7afeedte |

| Cousin | Translation | My cousin |
|---|---|---|
| Son of paternal uncle | 2eben 3am | 2eben 3amme |
| Daughter of paternal uncle | Bint 3am | Bint 3amme |
| Son of maternal uncle | 2eben 5al | 2eben 5ale |
| Daughter of maternal uncle | Bint 5al | Bint 5ale |
| Son of paternal aunt | 2eben 3amme | 2eben 3amte |
| Daughter of paternal aunt | Bint 3amme | Bint 3amte |
| Son of maternal aunt | 2eben 5ale | 2eben 5alte |
| Daughter of maternal aunt | Bint 5ale | Bint 5alte |

To say **my cousin** in Lebanese is not that simple. There is a certain structure to follow:

son of + relative + possessive suffix
OR
daughter of + relative + possessive suffix

Example:

Jad is my cousin (son of paternal uncle)       Jad 2eben 3amme
Sandra is my cousin (daughter of paternal uncle)       Sandra bint 3amme

## Text

### Practice reading and pronunciation

Ana fi 3ande 5ay w 2e5et, 3aysheen b nafes lbet ma3 2imme w bayye. 2aw2at minzoor jidde w sitte aw hinne byejo la 3anna.

Baba 3ando 2i5ten w 5ay. Ya3ne ana 3ande 3amten w 3am wa7ad. B3ayetlon ya 3amto w 3ammo. Mama 3anda 5ayyen w 2e5et. Ya3ne ana 3ande 5alen w 5ale we7de. B3ayetlon ya 5alo w ya 5alto. Wled 3amte (2eben 3amte w bent 3amte) b7ebbon ktir.

Ne7na ktir so7be kamen ma3 2eben 3amme w bent 3amme. 5ale ma 3ando wled bas 5ale l tene 3ando binten. Ya3ne ma 3ande wled 5al menno bas 3ande binten 5al min 5ale l tene.

5alte kamen 3anda sabe w benet. Ya3ne hinne bikoono 2eben 5alte w benet 5alte.

Ne7na 3ayle kbire!

**I have a brother and a sister; we live in the same house with my mom and dad. Sometimes we visit my grandpa and grandma or they come to us.**

**My dad has two sisters and a brother. That means, I have two aunts and one uncle. I called them uncle and aunt. My mom has two brothers and a sister. That means, I have two uncles and one aunt. I called them uncle and aunt. My cousins (son of my aunt and daughter of my aunt) I love them very much.**

**We are really good friends with both my cousins. My uncle has no children but my other uncle has two daughters. That means I have no cousins from from him but I have two cousins from my other uncle.**

**My aunt also has a son and a daughter. That means, they are my cousins.**

**We are a big family!**

## Exercise:

| | |
|---|---|
| Who is this? | Meen Hayda/Hayde? |
| This is my dad | Hayda bayye |
| This is my mom | Hayde imme |
| These are my parents | Hole imme w bayye |
| This is my grandfather | Hayda jidde/ jiddo |
| This is my grandmother | ………………………………… |
| These are my grandkids | ………………………………… |

Sam is my cousin (son of maternal uncle) ………………………………………

Layla is my cousin (daughter of maternal uncle) ………………………………………

George is my uncle (father side) ………………………………………………

Samya is aunt (father side) ……………………………………………….

**Answers:**

This is my grandmother        Hayde sitte
This is my grandkids         Hole 2a7fede
Sam is my cousin (son of maternal uncle) **Sam howwe 2eben 3amme**
Layla is my cousin (daughter of maternal uncle) **Layla hiyye bint 3amme**
George is my uncle (father side) **George howwe 3amme**
Samya is aunt (father side) **Samya hiyye 3amte**

## Verb Conjugations Examples

### Verb: To write

| Pronouns | Present | Present continuous | Active participle |
|---|---|---|---|
| Ana | Biktob | 3am Biktob | -- |
| Enta | Btiktob | 3am tiktob | -- |
| Ente | Bteketbe | 3am teketbe | -- |
| Howwe | Byiktob | 3am yiktob | -- |
| Hiyye | Btiktob | 3am tiktob | -- |
| Ento | Bteketbo | 3am teketbo | -- |
| Ne7na | Mniktob | 3am niktob | -- |
| Hinne | Byeketbo | 3am yeketbo | -- |

| Pronouns | Perfect | Imperfect | Bi-Imperfect |
|---|---|---|---|
| Ana | Katabet | 2iktob | Biktob |
| Enta | Katabet | Tiktob | Btiktob |
| Ente | Katabte | Teketbe | Bteketbe |
| Howwe | Katab | Yiktob | Byiktob |
| Hiyye | Katabit | Tiktob | Btiktob |
| Ento | Katabto | Teketbo | Bteketbo |
| Ne7na | Katabna | Niktob | Mniktob |
| Hinne | Katabo | Yeketbo | byeketbo |

> ➤ The active participle here exists in the Arabic language, however it is not commonly used in Lebanese Arabic.

## Verb: To draw

| Pronouns | Present | Present continuous | Active participle |
|---|---|---|---|
| Ana | Birsom | 3am Birsom | -- |
| Enta | Btirsom | 3am tirsom | -- |
| Ente | Bteresme | 3am teresme | -- |
| Howwe | Byirsom | 3am yirsom | -- |
| Hiyye | Btirsom | 3am tirsom | -- |
| Ento | Bteresmo | 3am teresmo | -- |
| Ne7na | Mnirsom | 3am nirsom | -- |
| Hinne | Byeresmo | 3am yeresmo | -- |

| Pronouns | Perfect | Imperfect | Bi-Imperfect |
|---|---|---|---|
| Ana | Rasamet | 2irsom | Birsom |
| Enta | Rasamet | Tirsom | Btirsom |
| Ente | Rasamte | Teresme | Bteresme |
| Howwe | Rasam | Yirsom | Byirsom |
| Hiyye | Rasamit | Tirsom | Btirsom |
| Ento | Rasamto | Teresmo | Bteresmo |
| Ne7na | Rasamna | Nirsom | Mnirsom |
| Hinne | Rasamo | Yeresmo | Byeresmo |

# Chapter III
## Vocabulary: Lebanon Survival Pack

### Basics (Kilmet 2asesiyye)

| English | Arabic |
|---|---|
| Hello | Mar7aba |
| Good morning | Saba7 l 5er/bonjour |
| Good evening | Masa l 5er/bonsoir |
| Good night | Tesba7 3ala 5er (Male) |
| | Tesba7e 3ala 5er (Female) |
| Welcome | Ahla |
| | Ahla w sahla |
| How are you | Kifak (Male) |
| | Kifik (Female) |
| How is your health | Kif sa7tak (Male) |
| | Kif sa7tik (Female) |
| How is the family | Keef l 3ayle |
| How is the work | Keef l sheghel |
| (I'm) fine | Mnee7 (Male) |
| | Mnee7a (Female) |
| | Mne7 (Plural) |
| Well (health) | B5er/Tamem |
| All right | Meshe/Meshel7al |
| Excellent | B jannin (It's excellent) |
| | Bjannin (I'm excellent) |
| And you? | W enta (Male) |
| | W ente (Female) |
| What is your name? | Sho 2esmak (Male) |
| | Sho 2ismik (Female) |
| My name is | 2isme |
| Nice to meet you | Tsharrafna |

| English | Arabic |
|---|---|
| How old are you | 2adde 3omrak (Male) |
|  | 2adde 3omrik (Female) |
| Please | Eza bitreed (Male) |
|  | Eza bitreede (Female) |
|  | 3mol ma3roof (Male) |
|  | 3mele ma3roof (Female) |
|  | Law sama7et (Male) |
|  | Law sama7te (Female) |
| Thank you | Shokran |
|  | Yislamo |
|  | Merci |
| You're welcome | Tekram (Male) |
|  | Tekrame (Female) |
| If God wills | Eza Alla rad |
| Really? | Walla? / 3anjad? |
| Yes | Eh/Na3am |
| No | La2 |
| Maybe | Yimkin |
| Excuse me (attention) | Ma twekhezne (Male) |
|  | Ma twekhzeene (Female) |
| Excuse me (Pardon) | Pardon |
| I'm sorry | Sorry |
| Goodbye (go with peace) | Ma3 l saleme |
| Goodbye (informal) | Bye |
| I don't speak Arabic (well) | Ma bi7ke 3arabe (Mnee7) |

| English | Arabic |
|---|---|
| Where are you from | Min wen enta (Male) |
| | Min wen ente (Female) |
| Do you speak English? | Bti7ke 2ingleeze/English? |
| Is there someone here who speaks English? | Fi 7adan hon byi7ke 2ingleeze |
| Help me | Se3idne (To Male) |
| | Se3deene (To Female) |
| | Se3doone (Plural) |
| Okay | Okay/Tayyib/Meshe |
| Look out! | 2oo3a! / Ntebeh! (Male) |
| | Ntibhe! (Female) |
| Ofcourse | Akeed |
| I don't know | Ma ba3rif |
| Where is the toilet? | Wen l 7ammem? |
| | Wen l toilette (French) |
| I understand | Fhemet |
| I did not understand | Ma fhemet |
| I didn't catch that | Ma sme3et |
| Sweetheart | Habibe (Male) |
| | Habibte (Female) |
| | Habibe is also commonly used for females |
| I love you | Ana b7ebbak (Male) |
| | Ana b7ebbik (Female) |

## Problems

| English | Arabic |
|---|---|
| Leave me alone | 7el 3anne (Male) |
| | 7elle 3anne (Female) |
| | Trikne (Male) |
| | Trekeene (Female) |
| Stop it! | 5alas! |
| Don't touch me! | Ma tid2arne (Male) |
| | Ma tid2areene (Female) |
| I'll call the police | Ra7 di2 lal darak |
| Police | Shorta/darak |
| Stop! | Wa22if! (Male) |
| | Wa22fe (Female) |
| I need help | Bade mose3ade |
| It's an emergency | 7ale tar2a |
| I got lost/I am lost | Do3ot/Dayi3 (Male) |
| | Do3ot/Day3a (Female) |
| I lost my purse/bag | Dayya3et jizdene/shanitte |
| I'm sick | Mareed (Male) |
| | Mareeda (Female) |
| I'm injured | Majroo7 (Male) |
| | Majroo7a (Female) |
| I want a doctor | Badde 7akeem (Male Doctor) |
| | Badde 7akeeme (Female Doctor) |
| Can I use your phone? | Fiyye 2ista3mil telephonak? (Male) |
| | Fiyye 2ista3mil telephonik? (Female) |

## Transportation

| English | Arabic |
|---|---|
| How much is a ticket to... | B2addesh l ticket la... |
| One ticket to...., please | Ticket wa7ad la..., eza bitreed/e |
| Where does this train/bus go | La wen biroo7 hal tren/bus |
| Where is the train/bus? | Wayno l tren/bus? |
| Does this train/bus stop in...? | Biwa22if l tren/bus b.... shi? |
| When will this train/bus arrive? | 2ayemteen byousal hal tren/bus |
| Where are you going? | La wen rayi7 (Male) |
| | La wen ray7a (Female) |

## Money

| English | Arabic |
|---|---|
| Do you accept dollars? | Bte5od dollar? (Male) |
| | Bte5de dollar? (Female) |
| | Bte5do dollar? (plural) |
| Do you accept credit cards? | Bte2bal credit card? (Male) |
| | Bte2bale credit card? (Female) |
| | Bte2balo credit card? (Plural) |
| Can you exchange money for me? | Feek tsarrifle masare? (Male) |
| | Feeke tsarfeele masare? (Female) |
| | Feekon tsarfoole masare? (Plural) |
| Where can I exchange money? | Wen feene sarrif masare? |
| What is the exchange rate today? | B 2adde l (insert currency) lyom? |
| Where is the ATM? | Wen l ATM? |

## Directions

| English | Arabic |
|---|---|
| How do I get to…? | Kif bousal 3ala….? |
| … the train station? | M7attit l trenet? |
| … the bus station? | M7attet l bus? |
| … the airport? | L mataar |
| … downtown? | Downtown |
| … the hotel | L hotel |
| … the embassy | L safara |
| Where are there a lot of… | Wen fi ktir… |
| … restaurants? | Mata3im? |
| … bars? | Pubs? |
| … places to see? | Ma7allet ta shoufa? |
| … tourist attractions? | Ma7allet siye7iyye? |
| Can you show me on the map? | Fike tfarjine 3al 5arita? |
| Where is the airport? | Wen l mataar? |
| Street | Taree2 |
| Turn left | Khod shmel (Male) Khede shmel (Female) |
| Turn right | Khod yameen (Male) Khede yamen (Female) |
| Left | Shmel |
| Right | Yameen |
| Straight ahead/infront | Deghre/2iddem |
| Towards the… | Sob l. |
| Past the… | Ba3ed l… |

| English | Arabic |
|---|---|
| Before the... | Abel l... |
| Watch out for the... | Ntebeh la l... (Male) |
|  | Ntebhe la l... (Female) |
| Intersection | Ta2ato3 |
| North | Shmel (just like left) |
| South | Jnoub |
| East | Share2 |
| West | Ghareb |
| Up | Fo2 |
| Down | Ta7et |
| Car rental agency | Shirkit te2jir seyyarat |
| Passport | Jawez safar |

## Taxi

| English | Arabic |
|---|---|
| Taxi! | Taxi! |
| Shared taxi | Service |
| Take me to ..., please | 5idne 3ala ..., 3mol ma3roof |
| How much does it cost to get to...? | 2adde l towseele 3a...? |
| Take me there, please | Khidne la honik, 3mol ma3roof |
| Pencils | 2 |
| Highlighter | 2 colors |
| Scissors | 1 pair |

## Lodging

| English | Arabic |
|---|---|
| Are there any rooms available? | Fi 2owad fadye? |
| How much is a room for one person/two people? | 2adde l 2ooda la sha5es/sha5sen? |
| Does the room come with… | Bteje l 2ooda ma3… |
| … bedsheets? | Sharshaf? |
| … bathroom? | 7immem? |
| … a telephone | Telephone? |
| … a tv? | Telvizyoon |
| May I see the room first? | Feene shoof l 2ooda bel 2awwal? |
| Do you have anything quieter? | Fi 3andkon shi 2arwa2? |
| … bigger? | Akbar? |
| … cleaner? | 2andaf? |
| … cheaper? | 2ar5as? |
| Ok, I will take it | Ok, ra7 2e5eda |
| I will stay for…. Night(s) | Ra7 2eb2a …. layele |
| Can you suggest another hotel? | Btonsa7ne (Male) Btonsa7eene (Female) Btonsa7oone (Plural) b hotel tene? |
| Do you have a safe? | 3endkon 5azne? |
| What time is breakfast/supper | 2ayya se3a l terwi2a/ l 3asha |
| Please clean my room | Please naddifle l 2ouda (Male) Please nadfeele l 2ouda (Female) Please nadfoole l 2ouda (Plural) |
| Can you wake me at…? | Feek (Male) feeke (Female) twa33ine 3al…? |
| I want to check out | Bade 2a3mil check out. |

## Eating

| English | Arabic |
|---|---|
| A table for one person/two people, please | Tawle la sha5es/sha5sen please |
| Can I see the menu, please? | Feene shoof l menu please? |
| Can I look in the kitchen? | Feene shoof l matba5 |
| I'm a vegetarian | Ana nabete (Male) Ana nabetiyye (Female) |
| I don't eat pork | Ma bekol 5anzeer |
| I don't eat beef | Ma bekol la7me |
| A la carte | A la carte |
| Breakfast | Terwi2a |
| Lunch | Ghada |
| Dinner | 3asha |
| Tea | Shay |
| I want… | Badde… |
| I want a dish containing… | Bade sa7en feyo… |
| Chicken | Djej |
| Meat | La7me |
| Fish | Samak |
| Ham | Jambon |
| Sausage | Ma2ani2 |
| Cheese | Jibne |
| Eggs | Bed |
| Salad | Salata |
| Vegetable | 5odra |
| Fruits | Faweke |
| Bread | 5ebez |
| Toast | Toast |
| Noodles | Sh3eeriyye |
| Spaghetti | Spaghetti |
| Rice | Riz |
| Beans | Fasolya |

| English | Arabic |
|---|---|
| Green beans | Bazella |
| May I have a glass of...? | Please badde kibbeyit... |
| May I have a cup of...? | Please badde finjen... |
| May I have a bottle of...? | Please badde 2anninet... |
| Coffee | Ahwe |
| Tea | Shay |
| Juice | 3aseer |
| (carbonated) water | May (ghaziyye) |
| Beer | Beera |
| Red wine | Nbeet a7mar |
| White wine | Nbeet abyad |
| May I take some...? | Please fiye e5od...? |
| May we have some...? | Feena ne5od...? |
| Salt | Mele7 |
| Black pepper | Bhar 2aswad |
| Butter | Zibde |
| Excuse me, waiter | 3afwan, garçon! |
| I'm finished | 5allaset |
| It was delicious | Kenit taybe |
| Please clear the plates | 3mol ma3roof sheel l s7oon (Male) |
|  | 3mele ma3roof sheele l s7oon (Female) |
| The check, please | L 7seb eza bitreed/bitreede |

## Bars

| English | Arabic |
|---|---|
| Do you serve alcohol? | 3andak ko7ool? (Male)<br>3andik ko7ool? (Female)<br>3andkon ko7ool? (Plural) |
| Is there table service? | Fi 5idmit tawlet? |
| A beer/ 2 beers, please | Please we7de beera/tnen beera |
| A glass of red wine please | Kes nbeet a7mar please |
| A glass of white wine please | Kes nbeet abyad please |
| A bottle, please | 2annine, please |
| Whiskey | Whiskey |
| Vodka | Vodka |
| Rum | Rum |
| Water | May |
| Pepsi | Pepsi |
| Orange juice | 3aseer laymoon |
| One more please | Wa7ad tene, please (Male)<br>wi7de tenye, please (Female) |
| When is closing time? | Ayya se3a bitsakro? |

## Shopping

| English | Arabic |
|---|---|
| Do you have this in my size? | Fi menna 3a 2yese? |
| How much is this? | B 2adde hay? |
| That's too expensive | Hayde/Hayde ktir ghalye |
| Would you take...? | Bte5do...? |
| Expensive | Ghale/ghalye |
| Cheap | R5ees/r5eesa |
| I can't afford it | Ma ma3e 7a2o/7a22a |
| I don't want it | Ma badde ye/yeha |
| I'm not interested | Manne mihtam/mihtamme |
| Ok, I'll take it | Ok, ra7 e5do/e5eda |
| Can I have a bag? | Feene e5od kees? |
| Do you ship (overseas) | Btish7ano (dowale) |
| I need... | Badde |
| Toothpaste | Ma3joon snen |
| Toothbrush | Firsheyit snen |
| Tampons | Tampons or fowat (pads) |
| Soap | Saboon |
| Shampoo | Shampoo |
| Pain reliever | Dawa la waja3... |
| Cold medicine | Dawa lal rashe7 |
| Stomach medicine | Dawa lal mi3de |
| Razor | Shafra or shafrit 7le2a |
| Umbrella | Shamsiyye |
| Sunblock lotion | Crème lal shames |
| Batteries | Battariyyet |
| Paper/s | War2a/wra2 |
| Pen | 2alam |
| Newspaper | Jareede |
| Magazine | Majalle |
| Dictionary | 2amoos |

## Driving

| English | Arabic |
|---|---|
| I want to rent a car | Badde 2ista2jir siyyara |
| Can I get insurance? | Feene e5od te2min? |
| Stop | W2aaf/wa22if |
| One way | One way |
| No parking | Mamnoo3 l wo2oof |
| Speed limit | L sir3a l koswa |
| Gas station | M7attit benzene |
| Petrol | Benzene |
| Diesel | Mezoot |

## Authority

| English | Arabic |
|---|---|
| I haven't done anything wrong | Ma 3melet shi ghalat |
| It was misunderstanding | Ken soo2 tafehom |
| Where are you taking me? | Wen 2e5deene? |
| Am I under arrest? | Ana maw2oof? (Male) |
| | Ana maw2oofe? (Female) |
| I am an American citizen | Ana mowatin amirkene (Male) |
| | Ana mowatne amirkeniyye (Female) |
| I am an Australian citizen | Ana mowatin austral (Male) |
| | Ana mowatne australiyye (Female) |
| I am a British citizen | Ana mowatin britane (Male) |
| | Ana mowatne britaniyye (Female) |
| I want to talk to the... | Badde i7ke ma3... |
| ... Australian Embassy | L safara l 2ostraliyye |
| ... American Embassy | L safara l 2amirkiyye |
| ... British Embassy | L safara l britaniyye |
| I want to talk to a lawyer | Badde 2i7ke mo7ame |
| Can I just pay a fine now? | Fiyye bas edfa3 zabet halla2? |

## Outro

I hope you have all enjoyed the content of this book and will help you reach the goals you are aiming for!

I would be happy if you would like to check out my further work on all my YouTube channels: MatarTV, MatarEducation and MatarPodcast.

If you have any questions or feedback, please DM me on Instagram under: MatarTV.

Thank you again for buying this book and I hope I was able to give you some kind of value.

Stay safe and....
Yo2borne Alla!

Printed in Poland
by Amazon Fulfillment
Poland Sp. z o.o., Wrocław